The Voice of God

PSALM 19:1-4

The Voice of God

Psalm 19:1-4

Robert M. Smith

Guardian BOOKS

Belleville, Ontario, Canada

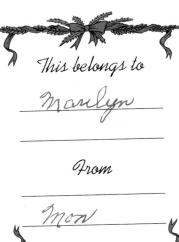

This belongs to

Marilyn

From

Mom

THE VOICE OF GOD

Copyright © 2002, Robert M. Smith

ISBN: 1-55306-418-6

**For more information or
to order additional copies, please contact:**

Robert M. Smith
49 Davis Avenue
Callander, Ontario, Canada
P0H 1H0

Guardian Books is an imprint of *Essence Publishing,*
a Christian Book Publisher dedicated to furthering the work of Christ through the written word.
For more information, contact:
44 Moira Street West, Belleville, Ontario, Canada K8P 1S3.
Phone: 1-800-238-6376. Fax: (613) 962-3055.
E-mail: info@essencegroup.com
Internet: www.essencegroup.com

Printed in Canada
by

The heavens declare the glory of God;
the skies proclaim the work of His hands.
Day after day they pour forth speech;
night after night they display knowledge.
There is no speech or language
where their voice is not heard.
Their voice goes out into all the earth,
and their words to the ends of the world.

~ Psalm 19:1-4 ~

Preface PSALM 19:1-4

Growing up in northern Canada was not as disadvantageous as most would imagine. It is true that, throughout my childhood and adolescence, I never knew what a pizza parlor was. I couldn't tell you what a nightclub was like. I knew nothing of major crimes and the subsequent paralysis they leave upon a community. A driver's license was a rare thing among the teenagers of my town! Staying out beyond the stroke of midnight did not happen very often. All the amenities we attribute to the "normal" life in big cities to the south were, virtually, absent in the north, but there were other things to experience. There was some "real living" to be done and lots of lessons to be learned.

As a young lad, my spare time was, usually, spent in the company of my dad. Because we lived in a mining town of 2,000 people with lakes and wilderness all around, much of that time was spent hunting and fishing. And when my family travelled as a part of the summer holiday ritual, we preferred to head for a wilderness retreat than be trapped in a city where we reckoned life to be merciless! Growing up with a love, knowledge and respect for nature was the result of wise, nurturing parents. I owe them so much!

Upon graduating from grade thirteen in tiny Cobalt High School, I was encouraged to attend business college in North Bay, Ontario. This city, of approximately 30,000 people at that time, was only 100 miles to the south, so I had the opportunity of hitching rides north on any weekend or holiday. My college years were a learning experience of another kind. The nightlife was something new and exciting to a young neophyte from the north. It caused me trouble both scholastically and personally during my first year: I just barely made the grade! But I had learned my way around, so my second year was easier to handle. Though I didn't discipline myself more, I was getting better marks.

During my final of three years at the college, I learned of a God I had ignored for many years. I learned of Someone who had given more to me—who had sacrificed more for me—than anyone else ever could or would! To that point in my life, I had been attentive to the requirements of a religion that told me a little bit about Jesus Christ, a little bit about the Trinity, a little bit about heaven and a little bit about everything spiritual. Therefore, to that point in my life, I was doing my bit to "earn" my way into heaven and a lot more to please myself!

Through the perseverance and the faith of a young woman I had known for many years, however, I was starting to learn more. Most of all, I was learning I needed a Saviour, for my life was not worthy of a place in heaven. To this point in time, I had been on a treadmill of self-indulgence. Now that I was finally on my own, I was looking for all the things I had missed when I was younger, figuring I owed it to myself. But there was always something gnawing away at me; there was a simplicity and a truth that I needed even though I didn't know why. This went on for several months.

Then, on a cold, January, Saturday morning in 1973—in a college residence—I got out of bed after wrestling with the truth of salvation in Jesus Christ all night. I was not sure why, but I walked over to the window in my room and looked out at a dazzling, snow-covered forest. I found nothing to keep me from making the most important decision of my life so, turning back towards my bed, I dropped to my knees! There were no arguments I could use against the Lord; holding Him at bay was not an option. I repented of a life that had been lived without Christ. I repented of my sin toward God, of my disregard for who He was and what He had done for me, of the emptiness and darkness I allowed to reign in my heart. Then, calling upon the Father, I begged Him that the sacrifice of His Son be applied to me! I poured myself out to Him for hours and, when I arose from my knees again, went to that same window and looked out once more. The scene that struck my eyes before was still there, but everything in that vista had been changed. It was no longer just scenery! It was no longer bereft of meaning! It was, literally, screaming out glory to God! Never had I seen such a sight! Never had I heard such a Voice! Never have I forgotten!

That year, I went on to acquire a business administration diploma and added a purchasing management certification and various computer technology credentials later. However, God had already given me the attributes He wanted me to use for Him throughout my life. From childhood, I had an overwhelming urge to draw and paint. Throughout my teens, I developed my skills as an artist by imitating other artists since I had no access to art classes. Such things were not available in a high school of 165 students! By the time I reached my thirties, however, I had my own artistic technique (brushed charcoal). I was preaching in many churches and publishing articles on faith. My pathway was becoming clearer, and the tools I possessed were God-given, not man-made.

Nowadays, there is a sense of urgency about the Church, with the Lord's return being immanent. I can feel it—strongly—and my sermons have taken on a different format because of it. The more I think of the methods used by our Lord Jesus to draw people's attention to the presence of God and His will, the more I feel a responsibility to use the gifts I have by pursuing the same methods as my Lord and Saviour. Time after time, Jesus took His disciples aside to teach them spiritual truths. Time after time, He pointed to lilies, sparrows, grass, ravens, seeds and other parts of creation to make a specific point. All of nature was established by a sovereign God and, therefore, all of nature could be used to learn of Him! The apostle Paul summarized it best when he wrote to the church in Rome:

> *For since the creation of the world God's invisible qualities—his eternal power and divine nature— have been clearly seen, being understood from what has been made, so that men are without excuse* (Rom. 1:20).

In his book, *My Utmost for His Highest*, Oswald Chambers captured the essence of what my soul feels:

> The people of God in Isaiah's time had blinded their minds' ability to see God by looking on the face of idols. But Isaiah made them look up at the heavens; that is, he made them begin to use their power to think and to visualize correctly. If we are children of God, we have a tremendous treasure in nature and will realize that it is holy and sacred. We will see God reaching out to us in every wind that blows, every sunrise and sunset, every cloud in the sky, every flower that blooms, and every leaf that fades, if we will only begin to use our blinded thinking to visualize it.[1]

Perhaps mankind has grown dull. Maybe our age has been so desensitized by hedonism in all its forms—from the television screen to the city street—that we have more trouble "seeing" God in creation than any other people in history. Or, perhaps, we are blind and deaf to the sight and sound of God walking in the gardens of the world because we have destroyed more of creation through the philosophy of evolution and our disrespect for natural resources. Whatever the problem, we are in desperate need of hearing mountains and forests "singing" and "clapping" and "rejoicing"! It is still happening. God is still there. All we need to do is to look and to listen!

Chapter One PSALM 19:1-4

There was a time when Ruffed Grouse were so plentiful in northern Ontario one could bring several home after spending a single autumn Saturday hunting. When he was a youngster, my dad could "bag" quite a few of these birds in one trek through the bush. In this way, all of the families of the north relied upon the bounty of the wilderness in order to survive, especially those families that consisted of ten or more members.

When I was a boy, however, the need for supplementing diet with wild game was not so severe. Most of my friends and the families in northern Ontario went hunting because they liked the challenge and because they relished the flavour of the creatures hunted. Though I'm not fond of food at the best of times, I have to admit there are few meals to compare with the extraordinary taste of a partridge stew! Thus, I was as preoccupied with the hunt as any other individual and, like other hunters, had to get to know my quarry as thoroughly as possible.

As time wore on, however, I became so enamoured with the beauty of the Ruffed Grouse and the spruce grouse I could not bear to harm them anymore. I had learned so much about them—their habits, lifestyle, enemies, problems—I simply could not kill them for food unless it was an absolute necessity. Of course, I haven't had any such necessity in over thirty years. The decision to turn from a hunter into a naturalist came to me because of one grouse in particular that ventured into my sights—quite literally, at my feet—while I was home from college during the autumn of 1972.

It was a gorgeous Saturday afternoon. The sun was bright and the air was full of that distinct smell of autumn leaves and plants that were shutting down for the coming winter. I had wandered to a hillside in the woods behind Bass Lake, and there wasn't another person around for miles. Toting my trusty, Savage, pump-action .22, a comfortable feeling washing over me, a young partridge (that's what we call them up here) sauntered across my path. It didn't seem frightened by my presence. Usually, during hunting season, they become quite skittish for obvious reasons. I could have shot him with my eyes closed, he was that close! However, I had a change of heart at that moment. I lowered my gun and made a feeble pretense of scaring it away, but it wouldn't leave me! So, I just decided to watch him until *he* chose to move along. That was a smart bird; he certainly knew what he was doing to me. He was a little angel, sent from heaven itself, to help in the transformation of my life!

I do not reprimand hunters or trappers because I have lived in the north and know how important it is to harvest and manage the provisions of nature in order to survive. Mankind has long been a part of the food chain and the balance of nature; to remove him entirely, instead of adjusting his ways, is quite possibly more destructive to the environment than any other action. In northern Ontario and various other parts of the huge country of Canada, there are people who use the bounty of creation properly; it is neither abused nor mismanaged. But as for me, I was meant to study and paint such things, not kill them. The environment is there for our benefit, and it makes perfectly good sense to treat it with respect and maybe even learn a few things in the process!

Now, the Ruffed Grouse is like a wild chicken. Apart from its ability to burst into a high-powered flight, its feeding habits and mannerisms are virtually identical to its barnyard cousin. The elegance of its plumage is both stunning and practical. With its complex pattern of browns, blacks and greys, it can render itself invisible by sitting still in underbrush, or it can look spectacular when on display or drumming (a beating of its wings to declare territory and eligibility as a mate). It is one of the most beautiful of all birds—beautiful in its design and in its character!

There are a number of things that set it apart from all other birds, however. One of these things has been briefly mentioned: the drumming. However, I am more concerned with a couple of its winter habits. Through these, we will see some amazing things that actually pertain to the Word of God. That God chooses to reveal Himself through creation is a time-honoured belief, rooted and grounded in the Bible. Thus, if we are careful in our observance of nature, we will always see truth revealed; it is a part of the very pattern God has placed within His creation. Every creature can tell us something about God and His plan and the Ruffed Grouse is particularly good at this.

During the winter months in northern Ontario, the temperature can drop to extremes of minus fifty degrees (Fahrenheit or Celsius doesn't really matter when it gets that low!). This can be deadly to many creatures in the wilderness. They have to make adjustments in order to survive and the Ruffed Grouse has a unique way of protecting itself from the wind and cold. In the evening, it will find an isolated section of the boreal forest and, after strutting out on a tree limb, it will dive headfirst into the snow. Snow is the ally of all creatures in the north (man included). I have, on many occasions, built shelters of snow to protect myself in the forest. It is the most adaptable and friendly substance a man can find: it can quench thirst, be made into shelter and even assist in capturing wild game! Into this friend dives the Ruffed Grouse.

This action has potential hazards, of course! If the snow has a crust on the surface, or if it is not particularly deep, the partridge can break its neck which is not very strong at the best of times. It would be like slamming into your living room window at full speed, and we all know what that does to birds! The grouse, therefore, gives us a prime example of faith! It exhibits more faith than the average person, for it can die in the exercise of its faith. We, on the other hand, have absolutely nothing to lose—and everything to gain—when we place our faith in Christ. Whether it is the initial faith of trusting Jesus Christ as our Saviour or the ongoing faith of trusting Jesus Christ as our Lord, we are in a win-win situation!

However, many people leave themselves out on a limb to face the hazards and bitterness of life alone without Christ! Held captive by their own fear, they perish in the night, never knowing

the comfort of peace with God and forgiven sins. Unlike our beloved little friend, when we dive into Christ for salvation and comfort, we are never in jeopardy. Jesus said:

> *"My sheep listen to my voice; I know them, and they follow me. I give them eternal life, and they shall never perish; no one can snatch them out of my hand. My Father, who has given them to me, is greater than all; no one can snatch them out of my Father's hand"* (John 10:27-29).

The message is clear enough! Who would not want such a position? The problem associated with accepting such an offer must come from a lack of realizing Who has said this! Could it be that the message of salvation is often ignored in North America because people simply do not have any idea of who God is? It is my firm belief that that is so. Therefore, just as in the prophet Isaiah's time, there needs to be a national wake-up call!

> *Do you not know?*
> *Have you not heard?*
> *Has it not been told to you from the beginning?*
> *Have you not understood since the earth was founded?*
> *He sits enthroned above the circle of the earth,*
> *and its people are like grasshoppers.*
> *He stretches out the heavens like a canopy,*
> *and spreads them out like a tent to live in.*
> *He brings princes to naught*
> *and reduces the rulers of this world to nothing.*
> *No sooner are they planted,*
> *no sooner are they sown,*
> *no sooner do they take root in the ground,*
> *than he blows on them and they wither,*
> *and a whirlwind sweeps them away like chaff.*

"To whom will you compare me?
Or who is my equal?" says the Holy One.
Lift your eyes and look to the heavens:
Who created all these? (Isa. 40:21-26)

It is not just in anyone or anything that man is called to place faith! The God of the universe is speaking to us, and He wants our faith to be placed in Him!

Once beneath the surface of the snow, the Ruffed Grouse teaches us something else. Being enveloped in the snow, it can sleep comfortably through the night. There are occasions in which it will leave its head poking through the snow's surface, but it usually buries itself completely. If you were to look for it, you would see nothing but a blanket of pure white! What a beautiful vision this is of the life covered by the perfect sacrifice of Jesus Christ on the cross at Calvary. God the Father looks at us and sees nothing but the beauty and purity of His beloved Son when we are *"in Christ"* (Eph. 2:1-10). No longer left to stand on our own before a holy, righteous and pure God, we are seen as spotless and as sinless as Jesus Himself. By faith, a Christian has a new, unmerited position before God; that's what is called "saved by grace"! The prophet Isaiah stated the intention of God long ago when he wrote: *"'Come now, let us reason together,' says the Lord. 'Though your sins are like scarlet, they shall be as white as snow'"* (Isa. 1:18). This ancient promise is fulfilled every time a lost soul comes to Christ and becomes a *"new creation"* (2 Cor. 5:17) bound for paradise! The action of our little forest friend shows us the responsibility of mankind to place faith in Christ; its winter resting place reveals our subsequent position before God (purified and enveloped in His love and grace)!

God is the architect and artist behind all creatures that reveal Him in various ways. The plan of God and His purposes are seen so thoroughly in the Ruffed Grouse, one cannot ignore the power of these spiritual truths. This is a lesson I trust none of us will forget!

© R M Smith -1999-

Chapter Two

Looking out on a bitterly cold winter's day to see birds flitting about as they search for food and warmth tugs at your heartstrings. Most of the birds seen through any window weigh in at only an ounce or two. They have bare legs and feet, no warm and cozy home and they have no medical plan! We are left to wonder how on earth they manage to survive in such weather!

Throughout the north, many people help wild birds through the winter by providing them with food. I like to offer birds the widest range of food I can possibly afford. This usually means I buy a birdseed mixture made up of peanuts, cracked corn, millet and sunflower seeds, a type of wild-bird food which not only attracts the greatest variety of birds, it also helps the greatest number of local species. And just so my friends the woodpeckers do not feel left out, I also purchase some beef suet to hang from the clothesline for them.

November is the best time of year to start a feeding program. It is most unwise to start earlier as you might be enticing migratory birds to hang around these northern climes too long. I have seen many species of birds perish or jeopardize themselves because of dependency on mankind and denial of their natural urges. Ducks have been trapped in ice and Hummingbirds have perished from hypothermia when they were encouraged to stay in the north by well-meaning people. It is also most unwise to start a feeding program without remaining committed to it. Such a program should last until the snow begins to melt in the springtime (up here, that may be until late

April), and a person should consistently make sure feeders are free of ice and snow and stocked with seeds. Dedication is the key. After you've seen some of these little "natural wonders" up close, you'll be so glad you started!

Every year, when I put out my feeders and hang suet, the very first visitors—without fail—are the Black-capped Chickadees. Without a doubt, they are the bravest of all the winter birds, never intimidated by the sight or size of a human! You can have them feed right out of your hand, and don't think for a moment they can't recognize what you are if you remain motionless! They land on your hand because they are brave, *not* because you are fooling them into thinking you're a tree! Being still for them simply gives them more courage and shows that you are earnest in your attempts to befriend them. This calm approach has been used by many to breach the gap between man and beast. The great conservationist of the early 1900s, Grey Owl, lived with shy and timid beaver families for years. "Horse whisperers" have shown what it is like to meet a wild stallion on its own turf in an unthreatening way. I have approached skunks, porcupines, moose and other creatures with this attitude, and I've suffered no ill effects. Don't be foolhardy though; just be respectful! Bears and cougars should not be on anyone's list of "approachables"!

My chickadee friends make winter enjoyable even when I am shovelling out my large driveway after a huge snowfall. It can be the worst of days, with biting winds and frigid temperatures, but, when I step outside, the first sound that greets me is the combined laughter of the chickadee and its relative, the nuthatch. The merciless northern Canadian winter is, at once, contrasted by these joyful sounds, and one's spirit is lifted beyond the ice and snow! What amazes me even more about these tiny winged wonders is that their cheery disposition on the coldest of mornings does not reflect the sort of night they had to endure! In the "deep freeze" of a northern Ontario winter's night, a chickadee must do an extraordinary thing. After finding a roost in thickly forested areas, and after fluffing themselves up to almost twice their normal size (an insulating practice), these tiny birds go into a state of torpor! Their body functions shut down. They are in a near-death state of existence.

In his epistle to the church at Rome, the Apostle Paul writes:

For the kingdom of God is not a matter of eating and drinking, but of righteousness, peace and joy in the Holy Spirit, because anyone who serves Christ in this way is pleasing to God and approved by men (Rom. 14:17-18).

Paul had, in this portion of his letter, been addressing the early Christian Church over the trouble that conduct had become. Some Christians were judging other Christians by what was consumed at the dining table. While some felt unrestricted by the Old Testament law, there were others who, not only observed the law, but expected fellow Christians to follow their indisputably good example! This, of course, split the young Church and created immense tension. I can imagine that worship must have quite often been traumatic; surely, this was nothing the Lord had any pleasure in! The coldness and bitterness these early believers were enduring did not, in any way, resemble the intentions of our Saviour's heart when He departed this world shortly after appointing all who were His to "love one another" (John 13:34) even as He loved each believer!

Paul wrote to both sides of this argument and told them what real Christianity was all about. He was an arbitrator; he saw the trouble both sides presented to true spiritual life. Then he indicated there was more to the kingdom of God than rules and regulations. Peace and joy, in and through the Holy Spirit, was of greater value to God than any observance or liberty found in any Christian. We have peace with God through our Lord and Saviour, Jesus Christ and are expected, therefore, to have peace within—not the kind of peace the world gives or understands but the kind of peace that surpasses temporal possibilities! As this takes hold in us, the alienation caused by tension and bitterness will begin to evaporate in our souls. We will start to exhibit a certain strength of character as the *"joy of the Lord"* (Neh. 8:10) wells up within our hearts.

But what is this joy? The Son of God Himself gives us the answer to that question in John's gospel: when we secure ourselves to our Saviour through faith—like branches to a vine—and make Him our Lord, we will have the joy of the Lord. Jesus said:

"If you obey my commands, you will remain in my love, just as I have obeyed my Father's commands and remain in his love. I have told you this so that my joy may be in you and that your joy may be complete. My command is this: Love each other as I have loved you" (John 15:10-12).

How do we remain or abide in Christ as branches to a vine? By obeying His commandment to love one another, and loving one another is putting an end to one's self for the sake of someone else. To put it simply, we must look to the example of the apostle Paul and even the example of our little feathered friends, the chickadees. In Galatians 6:14, Paul writes: *"May I never boast except in the cross of our Lord Jesus Christ, through which the world has been crucified to me, and I to the world."* Because of this, he can write further: *"For you died, and your life is now hidden with Christ in God. When Christ, who is your life, appears, then you also will appear with him in glory"* (Col. 3:3-4) The secret of life—true life—and the secret of how to possess a joy that transcends all earthly limitations is the mortification of self and the exaltation of Christ in us! *"For to me, to live is Christ and to die is gain"* (Phil. 1:21).

A while ago, I was led to understand this crucifying of self in an entirely new way. While having my devotions one day, and while also reading Krummacher's *The Suffering Savior*, the essence of this holy attitude toward life in each of us can be prompted, sustained and magnified if we were to fill our lives, our hearts, our minds and our souls with the final words of our Lord: *"Father, into your hands I commit my spirit"* (Luke 23:46). Take a lesson from one of the most delicate creatures on earth: take upon yourself the joy of the Lord and die to "self" for the greater glory of God!

Chapter Three

There are parts of Canada I have never visited. This is a gigantic country, and it would take several lifetimes to see and appreciate all it has to offer. Thankfully, however, our generation has grown up with the technology of television, and, although much of what passes for entertainment on the airwaves is trash, there are some informative programs to be seen. So, even though I have never been to the east coast of Canada (the Maritimes), I have had the opportunity of exploring it through a number of television programs and a variety of books. My favourite program about the Maritimes—and I have watched it a few times—is a documentary on the Bay of Fundy narrated by the noted Canadian naturalists, authors and photographers John and Janet Foster.

The Bay of Fundy is one of the most remarkable places on earth! Not only have I seen some of its wonders with the help of the Fosters, I have had the chance to study it—in depth—in high school. The highest tides in the world (a variance in excess of fifty feet) are recorded in this enormous bay (150 miles long and fifty miles wide). I have found that 3.5 billion cubic feet of water rushes in and out of this bay twice a day, and, at the site of St. John, New Brunswick, this torrent produces the one and only "reversing falls"! When the water rushes out of the bay, the current produces tremendous rapids (waterfalls even) that flow eastward toward the ocean. When new water rushes into the bay, the opposite effect is created, and the velocity of this onrushing water is so great it takes a speedboat to forge its way against the flow!

As incredible and astonishing as the water is, there are more incredible things to notice here. And one of those things is the red mud of the Bay of Fundy. That's right, the *mud*! The silt in this bay is so rich and thick one can sink up to the thighs in a fresh batch at every tide! This silt is, however, more important as a source of nourishment to the Fundy Mud Shrimp. This little crustacean is found only in the Bay of Fundy and in numbers that boggle the mind! Because of this little creature, other creatures can survive.

All manner of shorebirds traverse the east coast flyway in their migrations. The Bay of Fundy acts as a convenient "stopover" for them. They feast on the shrimp and then proceed, either northward (in the spring) to their breeding grounds in the Canadian Arctic or southward (in the fall) to their wintering home in South America. Of all the shorebirds that pass this way, the Semipalmated Sandpiper is the most numerous. A full 95 percent of all the shorebirds that visit Fundy are sandpipers!

Sandpipers provide us with our next lesson from God's creation. They are a mystery to scientists and naturalists alike. Even to this day, the scientific community that would have laymen believe it knows so much is left guessing at the wonder of migration. Ducks, whales, geese, caribou, sea lions, aquatic birds, song birds, sea turtles, fish and even butterflies confound the "experts" every year with the God-given sense of when to go elsewhere, where to go elsewhere and how to get there. All manner of theories have been brought forth—from celestial navigation to the use of magnetic fields—as an explanation for migration, but no theory has ever been sufficient to cover every aspect of the migration process.

Now if you think that is difficult, add this to it: the sandpipers that drop in to the Bay of Fundy for lunch on their way south and north do amazing things while they picnic for a few days! Thousands of these intrepid little voyagers descend upon the mud flats when the tide is out. They feverishly dart about as they gorge themselves on the tasty shrimp delicacies, and then, for absolutely no reason whatsoever, they perform an "aerial ballet"! In all the days of your life, you have never seen anything as riveting as this display! Thousands of sandpipers take flight in one huge cloud of avian bodies! Like a school of silver herring, they dip, dive, turn on a dime and fly over the shoreline as if they were one huge entity!

Extraordinary as that may seem, consider this: each bird in that cloud is receiving multiple— and *independent*—images through each of its eyes every 1/100th of a second! Let me explain. Most birds have an unusual (from a human standpoint) way of seeing the world. Because of the way in which their eyes are seated in their heads, two separate images are fed to their brains constantly (this is called *monocular* vision). Watch a robin, a blue jay, a woodpecker or some other winged friend as it is feeding, and you will notice this truth as they cock their heads from side to side, focusing with one eye or the other. Some predatory birds, like owls and some hawks, are spared this inconvenience (they have *binocular* vision) but birds like the sandpiper get these massive over-doses of optical information every moment of their lives. Now amplify the speed and the imagery received by each individual sandpiper in our cloud of thousands and it is no wonder scientists remain baffled! What a miracle this aerial ballet is when we stop to consider just one of the hand-icaps these birds must overcome to accomplish it! The reflex action required to perform such a stunt is beyond comprehension. Not only are they living miracles as they migrate, they are living miracles when they stop to have a group picnic!

Scientists do not know *why* sandpipers perform their ballet, and they don't know *how* they per-form it, either! If man does not understand something as basic (in our world) as this, how pathet-ic must he appear when he thinks about spiritual matters. As God confronted Job with the simple and profound questions of existence, He confronts us with this part of His creation.

Sandpipers fly, wing tip to wing tip, for the sheer delight of flight, moving as one, never crash-ing into each other, never showing "road rage"! It is a miracle that tells us of another miracle: the true unity of the body of Christ! Jesus left His followers with a parting commandment—a new commandment: *"Love one another. As I have loved you, so you must love one another. By this all men will know that you are my disciples, if you love one another"* (John 13:34-35) Any person who has become a *"new creation"* (2 Cor. 5:17) by the gift of salvation through faith in Jesus Christ (Eph. 2:8-9) has become a member of the *"body of Christ"* (1 Cor. 12:12-26) according to the Bible. As such, each member of that spiritual body has been given a direct command by our Saviour Himself. We are to show that we are His disciples by showing love to one another over, through and around all manner of denominational barriers, over, through and around all manner of personal barriers, over, through and around all manner of international barriers! The apostle Paul gave us a sound basis for establishing and maintaining such love when he wrote: *"For I resolved to know nothing while I was with you except Jesus Christ and Him crucified"* (1 Cor. 2:2). This is the essence of my salvation. It is the essence of my unity with all other believers, too. I may not always see denominational characteristics the way you do, but if we are "in Christ" and not just "in religion," we are related! And, if you are part of the family of God, I have every true spiritual responsibility to love you as a brother or a sister. This, of course, does not mean we have to be physically united as some have erroneously assumed. When I was in high school, my best friend lived on the other side of Cobalt Lake and yet we were so close you couldn't wedge a splinter between us. To emphasize the physical unity of the body of Christ misses the truth of our Lord's statements and promotes an element of syncretism. I am "one" with every true believer in China, though I have never been there. I am "one" with believers all over the world, though I've met only a few of them. I am "one" with the Father, though I have never laid physical eyes on Him. We joined the body of Christ the day we turned our lives over to Jesus by faith; we had full membership that day, and it hasn't diminished since. Ladies and gentlemen, our lives are hidden in Christ, our warfare is spiritual warfare, we seek a city without foundations. Though we walk this earth, our home is heaven. We are new creatures—spiritual ones!

We can perform a "spiritual ballet" in the body of Christ today, a ballet that can rival that of the sandpipers. Instead of showing disunity to the world by banging into each other, getting our beaks all bent out of shape and getting our tail feathers ruffled, we can show the world a miracle. True believers—regardless of denominational persuasion—are expected to fly in unison, and they have been given all the right equipment to accomplish the task. The best examples of a spiritual ballet in action are: bearing one another's burdens, praying for each other, forgetting about ourselves and seeing Jesus reflected in one another. When we commit ourselves to focussing upon the Leader of our flight (Col. 2:1-4) and adjust our flight pattern to His, the experts of the world will also be astounded by our miracle of flight!

Chapter Four Psalm 19:1-4

Mice are, perhaps, the most disrespected creatures on earth! Not long ago, if you wished to insult someone, you'd have asked if he/she was "a man or a mouse?" Insignificant, spineless, lowest rung on the ladder of life beings that they are, mice are slandered at every turn. Yet they are still around at the beginning of the twenty-first century and quite numerous at that. Ask any Australian about the staying power of a mouse, and you might come away from the conversation with a renewed perspective on these small animals!

I have had many encounters with mice, and none of them were boring. In our old home on Nickle Street in Cobalt, I was visited by one of the wee ones during the Christmas holidays. Never believe that old line, "Not a creature was stirring, not even a mouse"! I was only nine or ten years old at the time. My sister had a room adjacent to mine, my parents' room was just on the other side of the washroom, my aunt Rita was home for the holidays and it was late at night. In the closet at the head of my bed was a small, mouse-sized hole, and my Dad had placed some poisoned seeds in my closet to eliminate the occupant of that hole. Under my bed was a toy garage complete with instructions of how to build and play with it. The scene is set!

I never sleep well at Christmas time—too many things to think about, I guess. So, as I lay awake in bed this particular night, I had lots of exciting visions about the next morning and how I would get up the moment I saw any trace of light through the bedroom window. I planned my pathway down the stairs, contemplating how to sneak around those spots that creak and tattle on you! As I was making my calculations in the dark, I heard a little scratching sound under my bed. I have always been good at envisioning things, and I could "see" in my mind just what was making the noise and where it was. So, once again, I started to formulate a plan but it wasn't about Christmas delights anymore.

I knew the moment I turned on the light above my bed, the mouse under my bed would start running toward the hole in my closet. He may have had another hole somewhere else, but I was gambling he'd head for the one I knew about. My dad had also cautioned me not to pick up any dead mouse that might be lying around the house lest some poison should rub off on me, so I had to keep that in mind, too. I jumped up and snapped on my light. I heard its little feet scurrying along the baseboard toward my closet. Jumping from my bed and flinging open the folding door, I could see the little guy racing toward his refuge in the wall, and I lunged at him, careful to tear off a piece of the dry cleaning bag that hung there in the process. And, as incredible as it may seem, I caught the little guy! I could scarcely believe my good fortune! There, in my hand, was my new pet!

The commotion I created did not go unnoticed and, as I had awakened everyone in the house, I had to parade around revealing the trophy in my hand! When I showed it to my aunt and sister, they screamed and hid under the covers. When I showed it to my parents, my dad told me to get rid of it by—rather unceremoniously—flushing it down the toilet! I was shocked. How could he ask me to destroy such an adorable little thing? I was, however, not about to disobey my dad!

In the washroom, I stared at the tiny fellow while he swam around for a while. Dad was right; we couldn't let it and dozens of its offspring take over our house, and yet it was so cute to me! There was no happy ending to this story, however. When I hesitated, Dad called out to me in no uncertain terms, and I had to respond. In the life of a mouse, circumstances are more often cruel than not!

The ultimate prey of the predators on earth, mice seldom live longer than a few months. Their greatest weapon against total annihilation is prolific reproduction. Left unchecked by predation, they can become a curse! It is then they cease to be cute and frail. We need to know where they fit into life, and we need to learn that even animals as small and seemingly insignificant as these have something to teach us.

The White-footed Mouse of the Boreal forest has something extraordinary to say to us! It is a clever survivor, and it warrants our respect. When it is caught off guard and away from the security of its home by some arboreal mammal (marten, bobcat, lynx, fisher, mink, etc.) it performs a trick that is utterly amazing! If it is quick enough to get to a tree—preferably a balsam or a spruce—it will climb to the upper regions and then out onto the smallest branches. In its tiny brain is the knowledge that small branches will support it and not the larger predator. With deadly jaws only inches away, the White-footed Mouse will cling to the smallest branches quite literally for its life!

Christian brother or sister, do you go out on a limb for our Lord and Saviour, Jesus Christ? If you do, do you rely on the Word of God to sustain you? So often we think the verses we memorize and the concepts we learn from Scripture are miniscule when compared to the task of withstanding the enemy of our souls. We are keenly aware we are to be self-controlled and alert because our enemy, the devil, prowls around like a roaring lion looking for someone to devour. We know that we should *"resist him, standing firm in the faith, because* (we) *know that* (our) *brothers throughout the world are undergoing the same kind of sufferings"* (1 Pet. 5:8-9). Against such a powerful foe, we can feel too small. We can feel ill-equipped for the task. We can feel that words and faith aren't enough. We can feel like the mice of the world—prey for every predator and nothing more than food to ravenous jaws, spiritually weak and helpless beyond measure. However, we need only look to Jesus, *"the author and finisher of our faith,"* (Heb. 12:2 KJV). to see how words are indeed enough provided they are God's words and not ours! And faith is enough, provided it is faith in Christ and not in ourselves.

In Matthew 4:1-11, the Son of God shows us how effective the Word of God is in defeating the devil. Words may seem small and we have often heard that "sticks and stones may break my bones, but words will never hurt me!" Don't believe that old lie for the slightest second, my friend. The

devil cringes and flees when he is faced with the power of God's matchless Word. By using it to help us in times of temptation, or by using it in overcoming anything that man or Satan can throw at us, we are exercising faith.

As Calvin pointed out, "Our faith is really and truly tested when we are brought into very severe conflicts and when even hell itself seems opened to swallow us up."[1] Our faith is truly seen as faith only when it is tested. But where are the debaters and the philosophers of this present evil age? They stand before us—only inches away—with threats and the foolishness of man's intellect. Believing themselves to be wise, they have become fools for, as they bare their teeth to believers, they neglect to see their ultimate destiny bearing down on them from behind. The last enemy of mankind shows no mercy but, as we cling to what appears to be the little branches of faith and the Word of God, we are eternally secure and they are hopelessly lost! The devil and his allies in this world have yet to realize the truth of what George Mueller said generations ago as he caught the essence of Scripture: "Faith does not operate in the realm of the possible. There is no glory for God in that which is humanly possible. Faith begins where man's power ends."[2]

I would rather be a mouse in the hand and will of God than the strongest of men alone without Him!

Chapter Five

When I was in my early teens—and that was quite a while ago—my dad bought a piece of lakefront property, five miles south of Cobalt, Ontario. This acquisition was exciting for my whole family because the entire area was undeveloped at that time, and we loved the great outdoors. My parents were hard workers, and they expected my sister and I to do our share of clearing the land as well. On this property was an unfinished cottage with two small bedrooms, a tiny sitting area that looked out on the lake and a sink and counter with no running water. The washroom facilities were out back. It was a dream come true!

My dad and I worked at insulating and panelling the cottage because we could envision it as a perfect home base for fishing excursions (summer and winter) and for hunting excursions (fall and winter). When we finally finished our work on it, we were the first to stay overnight. Our nearest neighbours were a quarter to half a mile away, so the stillness of the night in the bush was overwhelming. Nocturnal birds and the peeping of thousands of frogs provided a background lullaby to enhance the sense of peace and tranquility that permeated the night air. We had a fire going in the stove, and we simply enjoyed each other's company until we got too tired to carry on. As the fire crackled away in the sitting room, we drifted off to sleep quite easily and quickly.

At daybreak the next morning however, I was aroused from my sleep by the most horrid alarm clock I had ever heard! If you can recall some of those old Foghorn Leghorn cartoons where either the dog or the rooster puts a metal dome over the other's head and then proceeds to hammer away at it, you'll have some idea what it felt like waking up in the cottage that morning! Right away, I knew what it was, and I could hear Dad getting up in the other room; he wasn't too thrilled about it either! He gave the now-cold stovepipe a couple whacks with a piece of wood and the racket ceased for a while. In about ten minutes, it was back again! I let Dad handle the situation once more. This time, he started to light a new fire in the stove and, after a few brief moments, we were rid of our early morning visitor.

The rat-a-tat-tat-tat we heard so long ago was none other than a Hairy or Downy Woodpecker hammering out a message on the tin stove pipe that projected through the cottage roof, acting as our chimney. At that time, we thought it strange for a woodpecker to do such a thing, but after reading about the characteristics of these birds we found this was not unusual at all! In sending out messages of availability as a mate, of territorial claims or of finding an appropriate nesting site, a woodpecker will select a tree that provides the most resonance. Our little "alarm clock" woodpecker found that our hollow tin pipe was ideal for his messages; he had probably been using this method long before we acquired the property! It was, however, time for him to find another way to talk to his friends and his rivals!

Of the 215 known species of woodpecker in the world today, twenty-two can be found in North America, and thirteen of those call Canada home. The largest species in North America is the Pileated, at over a foot-and-a-half tall! It sports a flaming red, pointed head, its loud squawks can be heard a mile away and it can chop huge chunks out of a tree with ease. As such, it has few enemies! I am always impressed when I see one of them clinging to the side of a tree in my backyard!

The Northern or Yellow-shafted Flicker is next in size at twelve inches. It spends more of its time on the ground—probing for ants—than it does on the side of a tree. The Hairy Woodpecker and the Downy Woodpecker look like twins, the former at nine inches tall and the latter at six inches.

Contrary to popular opinion, a woodpecker is not just another "regular" bird that happens to climb up and down the sides of a tree. At first glance, one does not suspect these creatures are vastly different from their songbird cousins, but take a closer look. There are so many anatomical peculiarities in these birds that they defy the theory of evolution. Gradual mutation (as the theory requires) from a perching bird to a tree-climbing bird is not possible because all of these traits would have to appear *at once* in any mutation of a songbird in order for it to survive as a woodpecker. Woodpeckers also possess a thicker skull than other birds, a brain that is surrounded by a cushion of air, massive neck muscles, a beak that is harder and sharper than those of other birds, special feet for clinging to the sides of trees, a special tail that acts as a prop, a special nose-guard to keep sawdust out of its nostrils and a tongue that is long, pointed, barbed and sticky to allow it to get at insects deep inside trees.

There is another characteristic that should also be noticed in woodpeckers. It is one that never gets mentioned but that a good wildlife artist should pick up immediately: the eyes of these birds are remarkably different than others. They are located closer to the front of the skull and they have a different "focal axis" (my terminology). Let me show you what I mean: take a picture of any bird other than a woodpecker and draw a line through the eye, from the "mesial corner" (where the tear ducts are located) to the "lateral corner" (the outer point where the upper and lower eyelids meet), and you will find it aligns with the direction of the beak of that bird. Now, take a picture of any woodpecker and draw a line through its axis and see what you get! Its eyes are adjusted to compensate for the bird's unique perspective on the rest of the world as it clings to the side of a tree, and the eyelids are placed at this angle in order to protect the woodpeckers' eyes from wood chips and splinters!

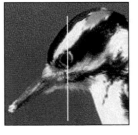 

These creatures are very unique, and their testimony to the Christian is also unique. Woodpeckers search for food and excavate their dwelling places by using their heads. When looking for a meal, they will briefly tap on a tree and then stop to look around… or so we think! They aren't really looking around as much as they are listening. With what appears to be seismic sensitivity, they hear the movement of grubs and insects within the tree after they give them a scare with their pecking. Once they calculate where the food is, they start drilling, and when they come upon a chamber or tunnel created by the insects, their long, long tongues wind their way through the tunnel to get at the quarry. Woodpeckers work hard. They listen hard. They stay focussed.

Fellow Christian, are you as diligent at studying God's Word as these birds are at their task? Many Christians read their Bible, and that is a good thing. But not many *study* their Bibles as often as they should, and that is a sad thing! Reading God's Word is like tapping on a tree to see if there is anything in it. You will know there is something important within because you can sense a bit of it, but you won't get ahold of it unless you do some more digging. Studying God's Word is like drilling and probing and searching for the very essence of life. *"Man does not live on bread alone, but on every word that comes from the mouth of God"* (Matt. 4:4). We need daily bread don't we? We need to dwell on, work over, wrestle with, meditate on, desire for and depend upon the Word of God just as much. We have to see that we simply can't go on without it, that we have no spiritual strength or life without it, that our lives are meaningless without it, that we are malnourished and starving without it!

Do you treasure the Word of God more than gold (Ps. 19:10)? Does God and His Word mean more to you than your job? Would you risk all in order to keep His Word?

When trying to snag a grub for lunch, the Woodpecker will place its tongue in a tunnel or chamber created by an insect. The tongue will then go in and around, up or down, through that passageway. It will conform to the passageway or it will not catch its prey. Do you let the Word of God guide you, or do you try to guide it? Do you study exegetically (reading "out of" God's Word), or are you in the bondage of studying isogetically (reading "into" God's Word)? Is it a *"lamp to your feet and a light for your path"* (Ps. 119:105) or are you wasting your time trying to use it in some other way? If you align yourself with it instead of trying to align it with yourself, the Bible will become all it was intended to be in your life! Study it and allow it to change you. Don't study it in order to change it and other people.

Finally, dig diligently into Scripture so that you become skilled in its use (Heb. 5:11-14). With *"faculties trained"* (RSV) one is able *"to distinguish good from evil"* by studying the Word. In our day, this is an indispensible tool. We are nearing that great and glorious day when Christ shall return, but, as we have been warned so frequently in Scripture, these days are fraught with corruption, delusion and sin. Without a true and deep understanding of the Word of God, we are of no help to ourselves let alone the perishing world around us. Let the Woodpecker be an example to you. See how it carries out the task the Lord has given it—vigorously and steadfastly working! In your study of Scripture, God expects you to do likewise, my friend!

Chapter Six

In the Great Lakes system are five enormous land-locked freshwater lakes. (I use the term freshwater rather loosely since lakes Erie and Ontario are anything but "fresh" anymore!) In my travels, I have been fortunate enough to look upon each of these Great Lakes, each one possessing its own personality through its own unique shoreline. The gigantic Lake Superior stretches out like an ocean from the rugged mountain edges of its northern coastline. Its icy waters are most inhospitable to swimmers and most treacherous to ships. Lake Michigan's eastern shores are clad with banks of pine forests and steep sandy slopes. It still provides sport fishermen with challenges and opportunities to add to their list of "fish tales." Lake Erie and Lake Ontario are the twins. They are linked by one of the wonders of the world—Niagara Falls. Their legacy within the commercial fishing industry is long past! Lake Huron is the home of Manitoulin Island, the largest freshwater island in the world. This island and the Bruce Peninsula define the border between Lake Huron and Georgian Bay. Although it is not usually mentioned among the Great Lakes, this enormous bay is almost the size of Lake Ontario! Every conceivable outdoor recreation takes place within its confines, all year long. It is also the gateway to what is known as "cottage country" in Ontario.

The Laurentian Plateau (also called the Canadian Shield) is one of the oldest and sturdiest geological land masses on earth, and it supports the entire Great Lakes system. This huge plate of granite engulfs Hudson Bay and covers 90 percent of eastern Canada. Within the "Shield" are vast mineral resources while its surface sports endless tracts of forest, lakes, rivers and wildlife.

Dotting the surface of Georgian Bay are thousands of islands, many of which are uninhabitable. They are either too small or too rocky to sustain a dwelling place other than the occasional tent. Although most of these islands can support no home or cottage, they are quite able to support grasses, wild flowers, shrubs and trees. Wind-blown seeds and even those carried about on the surface of the water often find a resting place on the rocks of Georgian Bay. The meagre opportunities to find good soil do not seem to deter most of the smaller and lesser species of plants; they are semi-aquatic in nature anyway. The trees are another story, however.

Of all the trees that can survive on these barren rocks, the pines seem hardiest. They have a way of overcoming the hazards of growing up on nothing more than rock! When a pine cone releases its seeds, they can drift onto a rock-island (some are too big to be carried very far by the wind, so water does a lot of transporting). They can get lodged in the smallest fissures of any rock. The first task of a seed is to establish a foot-hold, and it does this by means of an "anchor-root." The initial function of this primary root is not nourishment but, rather, stability and security! The root squeezes down into any crack in the rock and it often forces a greater cleft in the rock over time. The deeper into the rock the anchor-root goes, the better the tree's chance for survival!

Other roots are sent out over the surface of the rock. These roots hunt for food and find it in the soils that are being created by the work of the various mosses upon the rock. In many cases, the trees appear to have an "eagle's claw" system of roots as it spreads across the rocks.

To a Christian, this picture can mean so much. Within the pages of Scripture there is a "rock" mentioned frequently. In many passages, God is known as "the Rock" to the Israelites (1 Sam. 2:2; 1 Sam. 22:2; Ps. 18:2 and 31; Ps. 28:1; Ps. 92:15). He is known as the rock of "refuge" and "salvation" in other places (Ps. 62:6; Ps. 89:26; Isa. 17:10). Then, in the New Testament, the apostle Paul writes to the church in Corinth and states boldly that the "Rock" of the Old Testament (the sustaining rock that gave forth water to the wandering tribes of Israel and, allegorically, the rock that the prophets wrote about) represents none other than Jesus Christ!

The brushed charcoal painting I have chosen to start this chapter is called "Ephesians 3:17" ("rooted and grounded in love"). The root that a Christian places in Christ is one of love. It is the first root we have ever established in Jesus Christ (Rev. 2:4), and it is through this first love we maintain our balance and security in Christ. But we love Him because He first loved us. He gave us a cleft in Himself so we might take root! In the words of the old hymns: "On Christ the solid Rock I stand, all other ground is sinking sand"; "Rock of ages cleft for me, let me hide myself in Thee"; "He hideth my soul in the cleft of the Rock which shadows a dry, thirsty land."

Oh, how the strength of the Rock becomes our surety over time, rooted and grounded to stand firm in Christ by faith, to *know* Christ, to be filled with the love and purposes of God and not with ourselves! The apostle Paul uses these thoughts—and wants us to use them as well—to strengthen *"the inner man"* (Eph. 3:16)! This is not a "name it and claim it" salvation! This is not a success-hungry redemption! The Pine trees and the Christians are strong because of what *cannot* be seen. The branches, the needles and even some of the roots come and go over time. Storms and the elements ravage a tree as years go by, but the first love, the first root—so much a part of the Rock by now—holds the tree fast! Then shall we sing along with the Psalmist:

> *The LORD reigns.*
>> *The world is firmly established, it cannot be moved;*
>> *he will judge the peoples with equity.*
> *Let the heavens rejoice, let the earth be glad;*
>> *let the sea resound, and all that is in it;*
>> *let the fields be jubilant, and everything in them.*
> *Then all the trees of the forest will sing for joy;*
>> *they will sing before the LORD, for he comes,*
>> *he comes to judge the earth.*
> *He will judge the world in righteousness*
>> *and the peoples in his truth* (Ps. 96:10-13).

© R M Smith
- 2002 -

Chapter Seven PSALM 19:1-4

Every spring, northerners like myself are treated to a burst of life and energy as the birds of summer return to our environs from their tropical getaways. One fine day, before the snow has left the ground completely, the chirp of a robin will grace my ears, and a new season shall begin. Its sharp call stands out distinctly from all others! It heralds the arrival of warmer weather, longer days and busier forests.

Oddly enough, there is another bird that seems to appear just as early as our red-breasted songbird. It is a huge creature, standing four-and-a-half feet tall, with a wingspan of six feet or more! In flight, it is slow and laborious. On the ground, it can be overlooked because of its tendency to remain motionless. In a tree, it seems completely out of place, and yet, this is where it nests! The Great Blue Heron is a real-life enigma!

Not long ago, my wife, my daughter and myself were exploring the shoreline of Callander Bay—just one of the beautiful sections of Lake Nipissing. We chose to canoe an uninhabited section of this bay one summer's eve. The shore led to a very large swamp. The potential for seeing things like deer and moose is very good in this area; ducks, muskrats, beavers, ospreys, kingfishers, loons and cormorants are abundant here as well. Because these creatures move around a lot, they are relatively easy to spot from time to time, but the Great Blue Heron is another story!

With little more than an hour before sundown, the gentle, rhythmic gurgle of a canoe paddle slicing through placid waters can almost lull one to sleep. Among my favourite activities is the taxiing of friends and/or family around a lake or river. While they rest or simply survey the landscape, I can utilize the old hunter's stroke to sneak up—ever so smoothly—on creatures in or near the water. If no one is paying much attention to what is out there however, a few surprises can be in store for the occupants of our watercraft! There are many large fish in our vicinity that love to startle people by surfacing near a boat when you least expect them. Beavers, out of distress and sometimes in play, will warn friend and foe alike by slapping their flat tails upon the surface of the water (which usually sounds as if someone has just thrown a large flat boulder into the water). When alarmed, deer and moose along the shore will jump back into the safety of the forest and, thereby, create quite a commotion too. But the best surprise of all comes from the Great Blue!

The long shadows of a summer evening are perfect for hiding tall, stately birds in the midst of bulrushes and cattails. Blending with its surroundings—even with its great size—appears to be easy for the heron. When perched upon an old log or a dilapidated dock, it is still hard to detect because its secret to success as a hunter is motionlessness. I can imagine how its eyes must have glared at us as we cruised toward it, a couple of bungling interlopers drifting toward its favourite hunting grounds, unaware of the fact that this was *its* personal territory! The bird grows tense; it doesn't like intruders. Then it makes one nervous gesture, getting ready to jump into flight. That's when I finally see it, too late to show my wife and my daughter.

Rising out of a vast forest of cattails like some prehistoric monster, its wings blocking out the low sunlight, it announces its disapproval at being forced to leave such a good fishing hole with the most unearthly squawk! Each thrust of its giant wings lifts it higher and higher. Then it starts, slowly, to curl its neck into the familiar S-shape used when flying, and the dangling legs begin to trail out behind reducing "drag." What an incredible sight! What a wonderful reason to praise our God, our Father, our Creator!

The Great Blue Heron has one particular trait that warrants our attention. Although it is noisy and aggressive with its own kind, the stealth and patience it exhibits while fishing is extraordinary! Statuesque in every respect, it will stand waist-deep in a swamp, or high and dry on a log, watching for any sign of a minnow, a fish, a frog, a snake, a salamander, a leach or a tadpole. This bird's existence depends entirely on its hunting prowess. It is not a seed eater like many birds, it is not a great flier like the hawks and owls, it cannot outrun its prey, it cannot dig or scratch for it, either. God has, however, given this bird the ability to comprehend the abstract concept of refracted light and range. It knows when prey comes within striking distance of its long neck, *and* it knows enough not to lunge out at minnows or fish where they appear to be in the water. The fact that it is very successful in stabbing fish means it understands the refracted image of a fish is not indicative of its actual location! Amazing isn't it? And yet you will not find books referring to such things for fear these innate qualities will testify too loudly that there is a God, and that He provides for every part of His creation! With the tools God has provided, the Great Blue Heron does the most intelligent thing of all—it waits! When one of the aforementioned creatures haplessly ventures too close, the heron lunges forward, its dagger-like beak slashing through the water and its long neck extending fully. Then—successful or not—it will return, once more, to its seemingly-endless vigil.

It's never pleasant to wait for things, is it? Our society is so accustomed to instantaneous fulfillment that even the slightest delay can cause any one of us to lose it! In a culture wringing with leisure time and leisure activities, we are actually becoming less patient and more demanding. Where courtesy and respect once existed on our nations' highways, war has broken out! What would have been called the most blatant of interpersonal sins just a decade ago, is now tolerated and even, in some places, condoned under the term "road rage"!

Individual rights and civil liberties are the most important elements of our society at the moment. These words are designed to sound fine on the surface, but they are actually nothing more than a thin veneer of accommodation over the age-old sins of covetousness, greed and hatred! The current philosophy is: "If you see something that you want; take it. Your only sin will

be getting caught!" When observing such a philosophy played out in everyday life, I have concluded I must have been naive and a little hasty in thinking that the '70s and '80s epitomized selfishness. Nothing, in my wildest dreams, could compare to what the nightly news reveals to me during these first years of the twenty-first century! Where, oh where, has virtue fled?

Contrary to the tone of these last days is one of the most powerful virtues of the Bible, exemplified so marvelously by the Great Blue Heron. The patience of the Bible is more than mere waiting, however. The patience of the Bible—when it is a dominant trait in a Christian—declares that the three greatest spiritual attributes of all time have taken up residence in a mortal. Patience is the evidence, the outcome, the fruit and the by-product of faith, hope and love! It is also the virtue seen so often in God Himself.

We know that our Lord has taught all who love Him to *"seek first his kingdom and his righteousness,"* denying worry and anxiety (Matt. 6:25-34). In all of Scripture, there is not a more appropriate definition of patience than this. Yet, while many believers do not exhibit this element of discipleship, they claim to possess love, faith and hope in abundance. The Word of God is quick to point out, however, that this is not possible! Discipleship and patience are not two mutually exclusive terms. They exist together, or they simply do not exist at all! The apostle Paul readily backs this up when he writes about the nature of the Christian "walk" in Colossians 3:12: *"Therefore, as God's chosen people, holy and dearly loved, clothe yourselves with compassion, kindness, humility, gentleness and patience."* One of the indispensable virtues in a godly life has a depth that is seldom noticed: in one passage of Scripture, we can see the key element of both faith and hope is this rare quality of patience. The Revised Standard Version of the Bible puts it like this: *"For through the Spirit, by faith, we wait for the hope of righteousness"* (Gal. 5:5). Faith and hope are so much alike, aren't they? Even the writer of the book of Hebrews ties them together: *"Now faith is being sure of what we hope for and certain of what we do not see"* (Heb. 11:1). *By* faith and *in* hope we, mere human beings, reach into eternity. There is something beyond these temporal lives. There is Someone reaching into us, coaxing our spirits to look and seek (John 6:44). We *"wait upon the*

Lord" (Isa. 40:31), we *"stand firm"* (Jas. 5:7-11), and we look to the day when *"our adoption as sons"* is finally completed (Rom. 8:22-25). These things are "other worldly." To know their reality and power we have no alternative but to exercise patience!

However, to help us, our beloved Creator gave us one more spiritual pillar to stand on. It is, as Paul states, the greatest of the foundational gifts of God because it exemplifies His influence on any believer, here and now! It is the godly attribute that is *in* this world but not *of* this world!

> *Love is patient, love is kind. It does not envy, it does not boast, it is not proud. It is not rude, it is not self-seeking, it is not easily angered, it keeps no record of wrongs. Love does not delight in evil but rejoices with the truth. It always protects, always trusts, always hopes, always perseveres* (1 Cor. 13:4-7).

When he lays down the definition of love, Paul starts with the very same virtue that is used to also define faith and hope.

In North America, we have difficulty realizing the true spiritual meaning and value of patience, and it shows in the mindset we maintain. Within the last week, Gordon Fiss, one of the gifted young men within our Brethren assembly, spoke on temptation. He addressed the topic during a men's breakfast on a Saturday morning and then tackled it again during the Sunday evening service, less than thirty-six hours later. And today, I have discovered there is a crucial link between how we think of temptation and how we think of patience: we see them both as options in North American society. In trying to get a grip on how to handle temptation, we have automatically and unknowingly allowed ourselves to think of sin as an option in life. We set ourselves in the midst of serving God on one hand and serving ourselves through sin on the other. But the Bible does not condone such thinking, and neither does our Lord Jesus: *"No one who puts his hand to the plow and looks back is fit for the kingdom of God"* (Luke 9:62). The apostle Paul also states: *"But put on the Lord Jesus Christ, and make no provision for the flesh, to gratify its desires"* (Rom. 13:14). We are only fooling ourselves (and it is no joke) when we see sin as an option in Christian living.

Now, with regard to patience, we stumble with this same perspective. By continually thinking that patience is a virtue, we inadvertently classify it as an option. By allowing ourselves to treat it as a characteristic that may or may not be evident in Christian life, we have relegated ourselves to powerless living and a sham of spirituality. Patience is, indeed, a virtue, but it is far more than just that! It is the very essence of the life of God. When we believed on Jesus Christ for our salvation, He took away our sins, and (something that is so frequently overlooked) He poured new, divine life into each one of us (Gal. 2:20). With that life came all the attributes of God, so that we *may be filled with all the fullness of God"* (Eph. 3:19). And yet, we often think of this new creation as if it were a smorgasbord: we'll take a little of this and a little of that but none of that. We pick and choose the things we want for ourselves, never realizing that, the moment we start to do so, we loose the power and fullness God had intended for us in Christ! There are no options; it is all of what God is or it is nothing at all!

In Scripture, the greatest of God's many attributes is that He is "long-suffering." It describes His attitude toward the nation Israel and mankind in general. In this age of grace, the long-suffering God is the God of love, as well. It is no accident these two traits exist together in one holy and righteous God. If you dedicate yourself to knowing the depths of patience, your Christian walk will begin to take on a whole new meaning—the meaning God intended for all mankind from the beginning of time! Start looking upon patience as absolutely indispensible to knowing the God of the universe, and you will find the truth of what George Swinnock once wrote: "To lengthen my patience is the best way to shorten my troubles." When you treat it as something more than a mere virtue, patience will start to rejuvenate your spiritual life!

Chapter Eight

There is one animal in our forests I am grateful to have never met face to face! Studies have shown, and testimonies been given, to support the vicious nature of this creature. It looks like a miniature, chocolate-and-tan-coloured bear, but it will never strike terror into you because of its size. Weighing no more than forty to sixty pounds, it is not among the larger woodland inhabitants. It is, however, the largest terrestrial/arboreal member of the weasel family. By tearing its victims into parts and storing them away like a squirrel, and by marking its food as it would its territory, other creatures are deterred from scavenging its meals! Like its cousin, the skunk, it does not smell very nice. Unlike its other cousins, the marten, mink and otter, it is not particularly fast. Like its cousin, the badger, it is better left undisturbed. Unlike its cousin, the weasel, it is not a great hunter. Although it has these shortcomings, the wolverine has one overpowering weapon that ranks it among the most dominant mammals in North America: it fears nothing!

Trappers have dreaded and hated this animal for centuries. Being known for raiding traps and even chewing off a limb to free itself from a trap, the wolverine has no peer. A single, nasty wolverine can drive a group of wolves, a cougar and even a bear from its kill! As the ultimate opportunist, it can take down prey as large as a deer or take food from others. When it drops from a tree onto anything underneath, there is little chance of surviving its fury. Pound for pound, it is the most fearsome creature alive!

The fur coat of a wolverine is quite luxuriant and, unlike other animal furs, it does not retain moisture. For this reason, Eskimo hunters treasured it, and it is still considered a valuable commodity as a trim item on the international fur trading market. The most common problem with a wolverine pelt, however, is that it can be a bit damaged at times due to the rough and tumble lifestyle this animal leads! Being the ultimate vagabond, it never builds its own nest or digs its own burrow, and it has few enemies other than man. Some wolverines have been known to live for sixteen years, but it is believed a normal lifespan consists of ten to twelve.

For many years, I have longed to do a major painting of this unlikely subject. It is not very appealing to the eye with its dark earth tones and extremely plain pattern. One cannot present it in a noble posture suitable to the great hunters, or in a statuesque pose like some of the more graceful prey, but it has a certain wild quality that makes it fascinating. If I could bring out its intrepid character, I would be satisfied.

But what could we possibly learn from such an unlovable and unpleasant animal? It seems better compared to the sinner than the saint. Being possessed of every vile trait and a negative disposition does indeed present a challenge, but when I backtrack to the one feature that rises above all the rest, we have a spiritual lesson we truly need in these last days—fearlessness!

"Fear not" is a recurring phrase within the Word of God. *If God be for us, who can be against us?* wrote the apostle Paul (Rom. 8:31). Elisha looked out upon the hordes of the Syrian army surrounding the city of Dothan and seemed unconcerned in comparison to his distraught assistant because there was more than met the eye out there. A young shepherd named David stepped out of Israel's ranks to confront a giant, expecting nothing less than overwhelming victory. Although not particularly knowledgeable regarding seafaring, a small Roman prisoner comforted and counselled a ship full of fearful passengers, soldiers and sailors as they engaged a frightening gale for days on end. Three young Hebrews allowed themselves to be tossed into a fiery furnace rather than worship anyone other than the God of heaven and earth. A young son of Jacob did not succumb to the humiliation of slavery or imprisonment as he stood tall and confident in his Lord in the midst of treachery and neglect. The face of a young Christian glowed with peace and joy while a shower of rocks and boulders poured down upon him after he testified of his Saviour in the presence of those who had already crucified the true Messiah. After seeing such a list, we ought to be asking ourselves where this bravery comes from and how one acquires it.

Fear is a natural thing. I can remember, as a child, that I was frightened of the dark—especially the dark at the top of the stairs in my own home. One evening before bedtime, my parents tried to help me over this fear by offering me a bribe. When I was a little boy, a dollar was a very big deal, and that was my reward if I would walk up those stairs and into my own bedroom alone in the dark. After much stalling on my part and coaxing on my parents,' my dad decided to take matters into his own hands… literally. My hand in his, we ventured together into that vast unknown, beyond the reach of the living room lights. He took me to the washroom and turned on the light switch. We didn't race up there at ninety miles an hour and trip the switch on the way through the bathroom door like I usually did. Calmly walking into the master bedroom from there, we checked out the various hiding places where monsters had been known to lurk: in the closet, under the bed, behind the door. In my room, we investigated every nook and cranny; no darkness or semi-darkness bothered me as long as my hand was in Dad's! No terrors of the night could overpower him. Then we went back downstairs to try our little experiment again. And I failed again. I would not walk into the unknown without Dad.

Many times, believers are deceived by the circumstances of the moment. Things can look grim and threatening. Too many, too big, too strong, too inconvenient, too painful, too dark for me! "Why lead me there, Lord? Why put me through this?" There seems to be no point to it. Ah yes, but there is a point to it, and we know it, don't we? The point is to learn how to be fearless. Just like holding onto my dad's hand in the dark, holding onto my Heavenly Father's hand is the secret to fearlessness. We are *never* alone! We are *never* out of His hand!

Fearlessness is not foolishness unless it is outside the will of God. Fearlessness is faith worked out when God is the One in control! The believer's fearlessness is not as much bravery as it is trust.

There are two types of fear in the Bible: 1) terror, worry and anxiety; 2) reverence, honour and awe. Disciples of Christ are expected to know the difference between these and where they fit into the scheme of life on this earth. Every person on earth exists in one of the following states of fear: a) those who claim to fear nothing and do not recognize God as God; b) those who know of God but do not know Him personally; c) those who know of God and reverence Him; d) those who know intimacy with God and are living in complete grace and love.

a) *Those who claim to fear nothing and do not recognize God as God*

In his epistle to the Romans, Paul shows us when a lack of fear (in this case, "honour") is a foolish thing.

> *For since the creation of the world God's invisible qualities—his eternal power and divine nature—have been clearly seen, being understood from what has been made, so that men are without excuse. For although they knew God, they neither glorified* ("honor" in the RSV) *him as God nor gave thanks to him, but their thinking became futile and their foolish hearts were darkened. Although they claimed to be wise, they became fools and exchanged the glory of the immortal God for images made to look like mortal man and birds and animals and reptiles* (Rom. 1:20-23).

To observe our dynamic universe and fail to credit the Creator is the worst kind of folly; all other follies stem from it. The downward spiral of human depravity—personal, social, national and global—can always be traced to the denial of God. One needs no other proof than history itself, which shows the tragedy that man never seems to get his act together. Even in our modern world with our civilized attitude and advanced technology, there are those who claim to be wise and yet teach a type of animism that would embarrass the most primitive tribes on the planet. Worshipping self through the effigy of an ape is idolatry beyond that found among pagans, even in Old Testament Scriptures. Could it be God has "given them up" by now, seeing their minds and hearts are incapable of echoing the phrase: "Holy, holy, holy is the Lord God Almighty! The whole earth is filled with Your glory!"

b) *Those who know of God but do not know Him personally*

Of all the categories to be in, this one is the most frightening. The aforementioned state of existence, group "a," is usually maintained because of incredible ignorance; degrees and diplomas and doctorates are of no avail in that kind of blindness! In this second disposition, however, we find that a little bit of knowledge is a truly dangerous thing! There is a passage in Scripture so terrifying, I will leave only the reference for those who fall into this category. You may have some idea of who God is, you may know a little bit about what He expects of you (just as I once did), you may know you are not living up to those expectations, you may be avoiding Him and what He truly wants of you. If you are such a person, get a Bible—do not wait a single moment longer—and read this portion of the Word of God: Isaiah 2:11-22. Then I pray you will read this also: John 3:16-18 and Ephesians 2:4-10. The most grotesque error mankind can commit is not to honour and fear God. Man has placed such reverence in countless other things. And those things will be abandoned when the wrath of God breaks forth upon those who trust and rely upon them, but it will be too late. Don't let it be too late for you!

c) *Those who know of God and reverence Him*

In Acts 10:1-2, we are given the description of a devout, godly man who recognized God's existence and did all he could to get to know Him. This man was not a Jew but, rather, a Roman soldier. He lived out the truth written by the apostle Paul in his epistle to the Romans (Rom. 2:12-16). Cornelius knew of God, he reverenced and "feared" Him and he wanted to know Him intimately. This sense of "need" for intimacy stems from the initial knowledge of the truth that God is there. If there is a Sovereign over this universe, we are accountable to Him. Some people never get to this point in their lives. They search and search by experimentation, assuming the reverence God is looking for must be generated from within their own souls. Cornelius could have persuaded himself that he was "God-fearing" enough, after all, he did all the right things. His whole household (family and servants and associates) were affected by his devotion (Acts 10:7,24,27),

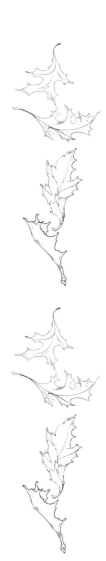

and *"he gave generously to those in need and prayed to God regularly"* (Acts 10:2). But God does not want our fear of Him to stand in the way of our fellowship with Him. God wanted to take Cornelius a step further because He knew the man's heart. God blessed this man by taking him from a reverence based on judgment and accountability to a reverence based on love. Love of God (honour and awe and devotion) can only come from a heart and soul touched by God; there is nothing of man's attempts left in them. Coming through this stage of spiritual development leads one to the beauty of the next.

d) *Those who know intimacy with God and are living in complete grace and love*

There is a state of existence that leaves one amazed at the wisdom and grace of God! In this state—defined best by 1 John 4:13-19—God takes up residence in a person's heart and soul. God determines to change mortals from the inside out. He wants mankind to live without fear of judgment; mankind was not created so it might cringe and cower before God but to have a loving relationship with Him. The state of fearlessness God wants in each person on earth can only be acquired by faith in the saving work of Jesus Christ (1 John 4:14-15). There is no other way to get it. No amount of good works, sacrifice and labour will produce what faith produces. No direction of our faith—whether it be faith in ourselves, our nation, other people or the supposed inherent goodness of man—will produce what faith in Jesus Christ produces. No fearlessness—no matter how brazen, bold and boundless—will ever be anything other than utter foolishness unless it is the fearlessness that comes from a deep love of God!

All too often, we are afraid of the wrong things and disrespectful of that which we should honour. Let the wolverine teach us that fearlessness is only as valuable as the one in whom we place our trust!

©RM Smith
-1999-

Chapter Nine PSALM 19:1-4

During the nineteenth century, there were still many bastions within the wilds of eastern Canada in which the largest of North American cats—the cougar—could be encountered with regularity. By the twentieth century, communities began to spring into existence because of the "pioneering spirit," the wealth of land-developers and the conquering attitude of industrial magnates. Man's dominance gradually pushed many of these larger predatory animals out of the East. Mining, lumber and farming industries contributed to this evacuation. Less than one hundred years later, however, these creatures seem to be making a comeback. No one is quite sure of the reason(s) why, but sightings of cougars have increased in eastern Canada. Some have speculated that the large contingent of pet owners is responsible, presuming that many former owners of the big cats have been releasing them into the wilderness because of the difficulties in keeping them. Others have conjectured that the western cougar has been pressing eastward with a remnant of genuinely wild ones already scientifically verified in Manitoba and western Ontario. Still others maintain that, because human populations and travel have increased, sightings have also. Whatever the reason, this new exodus has become an encouragement to conservationists and naturalists while also being a safety concern to residents, farmers and settlers.

Less than thirty kilometers from where I live, a cougar was seen in the summer of 1999. Not more than a kilometer from my dad's back door (120 kilometers north of here), one of them was sighted prior to '99 and, since then, a large cat has been scaring the daylights out of the people who live along Gillies Lake. Dad's nearest neighbours will not go out for a walk these days without bringing a steel bar along, not that that would help much if a cougar took a fancy to them. Of the two species (wolf and cougar) that are making a major comeback in eastern Canada, the more amazing return is that of the big cat. It is much more sensitive to the encroachment of man, and it is also the more intriguing creature. The cooperative nature of the pack, and the dog-like attributes of our lupine neighbours, makes them seem domestic while the feline is a more mysterious creature. I have encountered wolves in the wild at different times. Cougars, I haven't. Yet!

These cats have been called many things: "Ghost Cat," "Devil Cat," "Mountain Lion," "Puma," "Panther," "Catamount" and a host of other regional names. The mention of these, however, draws a certain picture for us… and it is not usually a good one. Though some have testified to their maternal and conciliatory nature, many ranchers and farmers consider them the ultimate enemy. I have heard stories of how cougars saved the lives of people lost or stranded. I have also heard stories of how they attacked and killed livestock and even people. Perhaps both sides are equally credible and viable—just as they are in humans.

Mature female cougars range in size from 100 to 130 pounds, while males weigh in at 150 to 180 pounds, sometimes tipping the scales at more than 200! With territories of 100 square kilometers per cat, it is not surprising that so few are actually spotted by human trespassers. Their overall length—from the tip of their noses to the tip of their tails—is in excess of six feet. They can run down rabbits and other swift creatures. They can overpower deer with one swipe of a huge paw. In the tropical Americas, they catch monkeys by leaping twenty to thirty feet up or between trees with ease. They can get within arm's length of a person before being detected because of their stealth capabilities. In fact, it is absolutely astonishing to think of a creature that is so "able" in so many ways and so beautiful besides! If I were to compare animals to the athletes of the summer Olympics, these cats would be classified as the elite. Bears would be the weightlifters and wrestlers, wolves would be the long-distance runners, Pronghorn antelope would be the sprinters and cougars would be the decathletes and the gymnasts! They can, indeed, do so many things so very well!

Another feature of this feline is that—due to its fitness level—it can live in any region of the western hemisphere, as efficient in the mountains as it is on the plains, thriving in the tropical rainforest and the boreal forest, just as comfortable in a tree as on the ground, dealing equally well with the harshness of northern winter and the harshness of desert sun.

The wild ones are all muscle. There is not a more physically fit creature walking this earth! And that sends a very important message to us. How fit, how spiritually fit are we? When a task from the Lord arrives at our doorstep, do we have the right tools for the job *and*, if we do have those tools, are we capable of using them to their fullest?

In order to be fit on a personal, physical level, we must be concerned about what we consume for nourishment, and we must be concerned about the exercise we obtain. If one were to spend all his/her time eating junk food like chocolate bars, chips and soda pop, all of the best exercises on earth will not be of any value. Similarly, if one were to choose a regimen of the easiest exercises known to mankind, the best nutritional habits would be of little use! These parameters are just as significant on a spiritual plane. One must realize that we are always consuming things spiritually: every word spoken to us, every thought that crosses our mind, every thing we perceive has some spiritual connotation. We are taking things in every moment of the day. These things, thoughts, concepts or ideas feed us and, thereby, nourish us—negatively or positively. In the same manner, what we involve ourselves with—the pursuits of our lives, the main thrusts of our existence—are spiritual exercises that we commit ourselves to. What we consume spiritually and the activities we are involved in, determine our spiritual fitness levels! To feed one's mind with steady doses of television, tabloid nonsense or inane novels will result only in stunted and distorted perspectives void of anything good for our Lord. To focus all our energies upon occupations that are secular in nature—successful careers, amassing fortunes, the pursuit of sports, the

drive for fame—will also make us spiritual weaklings. If we are to be of any use to Christ, we must fill ourselves with the right things and be involved in the right activities as we work out what we take in! Your mind must be challenged and stretched, just as your muscles must. The gateway to your soul is your mind, and it must be disciplined, fed and guided, or it will become lethargic and anemic. That is why the Scriptures even point out that we are to *"take every thought captive to Christ"* (2 Cor. 10:5-6). Nothing is to be overlooked, and nothing is to be squandered as we strive to do the will of God.

If you ever get the opportunity—through nature videos or in real life—watch a cougar or any of the big cats of the world as they chase their prey. Although their legs and bodies go through all sorts of contortions, twists and turns, their heads remain fixed and their eyes never leave their quarry! This is, perhaps, the greatest example for a Christian regarding singleness of thought and intent in prayer. James puts it this way:

> *If any of you lacks wisdom, he should ask God, who gives generously to all without finding fault, and it will be given to him. But when he asks, he must believe and not doubt, because he who doubts is like a wave of the sea, blown and tossed by the wind. That man should not think he will receive any-thing from the Lord; he is a double-minded man, unstable in all he does* (Jas. 1:5-8).

Christian faith in prayer also involves the mind, and such prayer should be full of the intensity and determination seen in a big cat; with chaos and unstable circumstances all about us, there should be a "one-track mind" approach when entering the presence of God in prayer. When seeking God's attention, do so without wavering. Don't let your head go bouncing around, and never take your eyes off of the Holy Lord who saved you. Our prayer life was meant to be powerful and beautiful. If it is not so, we have only ourselves to blame.

The apostle Paul at one point compared himself to an athlete. He saw that his spiritual life was in need of fitness as much as any athlete; in fact, a Christian's spiritual life is in need of fitness *more* than any athlete! Earthly garlands are nothing in comparison to eternal security and divine reward. But how does one work out (Phil. 2:12) in a spiritual way, and on what areas does one work?

Paul tells us that we are to *"buffet"* ourselves (1 Cor. 9:27), to discipline ourselves, to deny the flesh that wars against the spirit (Gal. 5:16-17), to lay aside every weight (Heb. 12:1) that can so easily hold us back from *"running the race"* (2 Tim. 4:7). These are the exercises—the answer to *how* one does a spiritual workout. It is the surrender—the forfeiting of one's own will for a total commitment to God's will. It is the mortifying of personal desires and plans in order to see divine life exhibited in mortal creatures such as ourselves.

Now, wondering about what areas of life to work on is tantamount to asking what the ultimate purpose of man happens to be, isn't it? If we know what is expected of us, we will consequently know where we need to concentrate our efforts in order to accomplish the greatest good. There are some lopsided perspectives out there, however: they often leave believers as unbalanced as a bodybuilder who focuses only on one part of his body. Any time you are faced with a teaching that claims to be "the missing ingredient" in Christianity, watch out! You may not be acquiring the fitness you seek, and your spiritual life could become as distorted as a bodybuilder with massive arms and a skinny body!

Some feel that there should be more evidence of the miraculous in a believer's life, and they bring all of their energies to bear on this. To be without signs, wonders, visions and earth-shaking events is perceived as inferior Christianity. The Bible does not give us that perspective, however. A simple reading of it is sufficient to testify that God is more concerned with being present in mortal lives as Lord than as a miracle provider. Do not misunderstand: He *can and does* provide, but that is not the real issue. If He never presented a miracle to you, would that change your submission to Him? Would He be any less than who and what He is if He doesn't deliver to and for you? No, a thousand times, no! We are to place Him above all else in our lives, not because of what He gives us, not because of how powerful He is, but because of *who* He is! He is the great and wonder-working God, and our lives are neither measured by, nor dependent

upon, the presence of signs and wonders. They are completely established by faith, regardless of consequence. A.W. Tozer put it this way:

> But the God we must see is not the utilitarian God who is having such a run of popularity today, who's chief claim to men's attention is His ability to bring them success in their various undertakings and who for that reason is being cajoled and flattered by everyone who wants a favor. The God we must learn to know is the Majesty in the heavens, God the Father Almighty, Maker of heaven and earth, the only wise God our Saviour.[1]

If you have any doubt about this, simply look at the life of Noah. When the greatest worldwide catastrophe of all time occurred, he lived hundreds of years just *being* what God wanted him to be, steadily hammering out the mundane and rudimentary tasks set before him. One huge event epitomized his life's work but, to that point in time, nothing but faith. Nothing but complete, unreserved trust in God, not because of what God was doing or how God was manifesting Himself, just, simply, for who God is.

Jesus Himself gave us the ultimate purpose of man when He quoted the Old Testament in response to the question, "Which is the greatest commandment?" Without hesitation, He stated the spiritual fitness level expected of all mankind: to *"Love the Lord, your God, with all your heart and with all your soul and with all your mind and with all your strength... (and to) love your neighbour as yourself"* (Mark 12:28-31). I'm sure that, if there was something more important than this, Jesus would have pointed it out then and there. He was, however, more concerned about what we are and what we become than what we do: the latter will always work its way out of the former but never vise-versa. Any concentration upon externals (good works, signs, wonders, visions, accomplishments, gifts, etc.) will be counterproductive to true spiritual fitness. Paul's letters warn about that often enough!

To be fit for the kingdom of heaven, the instructions are clear! To love Christ and to walk with Him is everything; all else is waste! By taking Christ's yoke upon him, the apostle Paul could say he was capable of being content in all situations, whether the blazing sun, the cold of night, on the mountain top or in the valley! If your focus is on anything—even those things that are good—other than God and God alone, there will come a day when you will not be able to rise to the task laid before you. Don't let that happen. Don't waste time, energy and life on peripheral things. Center on Christ and have Christ as your center, and you will be as fit as a lion for the service of our King!

Chapter Ten

When I was young and still living with my parents at Gillies Lake, the winters were always picture-postcard beautiful. Outside the huge window in our living room stretched a thick blanket of white, soft and billowy. The spruce trees that crossed the front yard, halfway to the lakeshore, were decked with mounds of cottony snow. On the left side of our property was a massive wall of trees creating a boreal atmosphere. From the shoreline, the snow and ice spread out over the bay in a perfect, unblemished sheet to the trees and rocks on the distant shore. Other than our house, there was not another man-made object in sight! But right in front of the window was a lone cluster of birch trees blocking the view somewhat. It stands there still. And in that group of trees, my parents decided to place a bird feeder which would afford us the opportunity of watching our little feathered friends up close.

One wintery Saturday, we were surprised to see something other than birds in our feeder! With the largest eyes you could imagine on such a tiny body, this little ball of fur was helping itself to the seeds. For several days, this peculiar little visitor puzzled us. It would arrive in the early morning, eat some of the birdseed, then climb up the tree and not come down again. My dad and I went outside to see if we could tell where the little guy went, but we could never find a trace of it. The little fellow was a magician. He'd appear in the tree and disappear from the tree, never leaving a trail. After a few days and a bit of research, however, I managed to solve the riddle: it was a flying squirrel! We had never seen one before and, like most people, we were fooled by his looks and antics.

The flying squirrel is the smallest of the Tree Squirrel family, weighing in at two to three ounces. Its enlarged eyes are evidence of its nocturnal habits; to see one during daylight hours is an extremely rare occurrence. This tiny rodent has a flap of fur-covered skin extending from the "wrist" on its forelegs to the "ankle" on its hind legs, and, with it, he can glide from tree to tree. That's how he performed his Houdini impression in our birch tree!

He is only one branch of the squirrel family tree, however. The squirrel family is quite amazing, actually. They do not hibernate like their cousins, the chipmunks and woodchucks. Their winter activities include reclaiming their caches of food as well as the mating chase of December/January. The only time a squirrel will slow down in the winter is to eat seeds of its own, to eat your bird seeds or to scold you from a safe perch! Their agility is legendary, and they can often be witnessed leaping from tree to tree. They possess highly-developed, specialized muscles and bone structures that allow them to perform their amazing tree-climbing antics. With double-jointed hind legs that can rotate 180 degrees, they can descend from trees head-first.

Although they seem to be cranky, noisy, selfish little individuals, much of what they do in the forest is communal in its effects. When working diligently during the autumn months, they do not realize it, but they are working for other creatures, too. The Northern Fox Squirrel forages for seeds and nuts, burying them all over the forest floor. These thousands of little caches then provide food for it, other squirrels, mice, raccoons and even bears. During the winter months, squirrels also build snow tunnels that provide miniature highways for many small creatures like mice, voles and weasels. Even the Red Squirrel—who stashes his food supply in one place and territorially defends it—can be a community-minded individual because, of the forty to sixty nuts it buries every hour, many will be left to sprout into young trees! Thus, these little guys can be bread winners and gardeners to a whole slew of creatures and plants.

These things remind me of what it is like to work with the Bible, to store up the Word of God in our hearts and use it for our own good and the good of others. Every Christian is to treasure the Scriptures, and part of that love is to memorize and utilize it in life, not for our good only, but for the good of all mankind.

Many years ago, one of the sermons I was called upon to preach found its impetus from within the seldom-used pages of the minor prophets of the Old Testament. In Amos 8:11-12, we read this:

> *"The days are coming," declares the Sovereign LORD,*
> > *"when I will send a famine through the land—*
> *not a famine of food or a thirst for water,*
> > *but a famine of hearing the words of the LORD.*
> *Men will stagger from sea to sea*
> > *and wander from north to east,*
> *searching for the word of the LORD,*
> > *but they will not find it."*

No matter what circles you choose—government circles, social circles, religious circles, international circles—you will find a desperate need for moral positivism, spiritual renewal and a knowledge of God. Our current secular society reflects spiritual famine with countless godless lives, more and more corruption at every level, a lost sense of reality and social structures that seem to be careening out of control. This, of course, has not caught God unawares. In 2 Timothy 3:1-9, we can read about the twentieth century and beyond. We could spend a lot of time and space on the woes of our era, but there is one major concern in this whole scenario that needs to be addressed above all others. Just as in Amos' time, the famine of the Word of God felt in the society was caused by those who had the Word of God and did not live it or share it. If we are continually chattering (like squirrels) and condemning the world at our doorstep without living a Christlike life under the power and the authority of the Word of God, we are the cause of the famine of the Word of God in our time!

If we have the audacity to call ourselves Christians, we have a responsibility not to defame the precious name of our Lord by our conduct! If we call ourselves Christians, we must be properly related to God: saved by the blood of Jesus Christ, sanctified or set apart for Him in life, discipled to Him with a dependence upon Him for our lives and a desire to seek only His will. If we call ourselves Christians, we must transmit Christ. Christianity is not a bunch of "do's and don't's," nor is it made up of Christians and their lifestyles. If we call ourselves Christians, we must be lovers of God's Word, studying it, heeding it and applying it before we dictate it. If we call ourselves Christians, we must be honest, facing up to our responsibility towards God (Matt. 22:37), facing up to our responsibility toward one another (John 15:17) and facing up to our responsibility toward the secular world (Matt. 22:39).

All words are like seeds: we take a thought from our minds, verbalize it and it becomes a "seed" in someone else's mind. These seeds can grow into fruitful plants which cause other people to grow and flourish, setting them free. Or these seeds can be nothing more than weeds that clog another's mind and heart with discord and bondage. Our words can show that we are dead inside or that life exists within our frame, no matter how feeble the frame may be. Words are spiritual things; they are never just words or noises in the air! Therefore, how we use them and how we back them up is of the greatest importance. How we filter our own thoughts and words is as significant as how we filter those we hear. The filter we are to use works both ways. It is none other than Christ (2 Cor. 10:5)! If what we are saying or what we are hearing does not measure up to the standard of a Christ-like life, it has no right to be uttered or heard and heeded by us.

In John's gospel, Jesus Christ was called "the Word." Everything God the Father ever wanted to say to mankind was said through Christ: the Father thought it, and Jesus said it through every motion, deed, utterance and implication. Jesus' words were delivered with authority (Luke 4:31-32). The things our Saviour said were *"spirit and life"* (John 6:63); they weren't just full of spirit and life, they *were* spirit and life! Why? Because He spoke under the Father's authority (John 14:10; John 8:28). There was power in the words of Jesus, the same power resident in them at the dawn of creation! No one who ever heard Him could avoid noticing that. He was never at a loss for words, knowing what to say and when to say it. Jesus never "rambled on" at any time: He would make a point and then leave it with those who heard. Their response to what they heard was entirely up to them. If they had "ears to hear" and "eyes to see," light and life would come to them! If they would not listen, darkness would be their dwelling place. Our Lord never pleaded for understanding or begged people to react favourably toward Him. When gentleness was required by the poor and infirm, He gave it; when a challenge and a reprimand was in order for the proud and religious, He delivered that, too. Not a single word fell out of place from His mouth. He said only what should be said. He said only what the Father wanted Him to say. The entire character of the Godhead stood behind everything Jesus did.

Now, consider the legacy He left us: *"A student is not above his teacher, nor a servant above his master. It is enough for the student to be like his teacher, and the servant like his master"* (Matt. 10:24-25). There has been much lamentation about the times in which we live. Many horrible things have happened because God has been neglected throughout the entire fabric of our cultures. The nightmares of New York, Kosovo and Littleton, Colorado are prevailing, while well-meaning Christians are pointing fingers at governments, school boards and justice systems saying it is because God is not recognized, honoured or glorified in them. This is most certainly true. The godlessness of authorities will always translate into a godless society; any student of the Bible can figure that out! But the point I have been working on in this chapter is that the problem does not originate with the authorities. The Church should be influencing society, not the other way around. Remember your Bible history! In the first century AD (for that matter, in the first several centuries AD), God was not recognized in governments, schools or the judicial systems of the day. And that never stopped the Spirit of God! Hordes of people were saved from a lost eternity while the governments were not only godless in their perspective, they were downright antagonistic toward the Creator and His beloved Son. Griping and whining about circumstances was not a part of the agenda of the early Church. They had more important things to do! As I write this, I am remind-

ed of a book I read many years ago. John Pollock took upon himself the task of encapsulating the life of the apostle Paul and, in a book that is now tattered from use, Mr. Pollock succeeded in defining the spiritual drive and dedication of the greatest evangelist of all time. The book itself is tremendous and I highly recommend it to all, but it is not the contents of this book I thought of just now, it is the title. The title delineates what we should be and what our God-given task is. The title is, *The Man Who Shook the World*![1] Are we letting the world shake and shape us? Are we letting the darkness give us a fright? Are we pointing fingers at establishments and people who are dead in trespasses and sins, expecting them to shape-up and live for God? Are we spending all our time and energy keeping the treasure of the ages to ourselves like misers? What are we living for? If the Word of God is not being seen and heard, we must face the reality that it is our problem and not the problem of those around us!

We are called upon to plant the Word of God in this world so it might not starve to death. Our diligence in this vocation must stem from character and integrity beyond reproach. Therefore, only by taking the Sovereign authority of God into our own hearts and lives will we be able to fulfill this mandate!

© B.M. Smith
-1999-

Chapter Eleven Psalm 19:1-4

In the summer of 1999, our chapel held some picnics in the city park after services on Sunday afternoons. It is a treat to get together over a simple meal and not have to worry about spilling anything on the carpet! It is also a treat to gather with more friends than one could jam into his/her own home for a meal and fellowship. At these picnics, the children can practically run ragged as long as they do not disturb other picnickers, but every now and then one feels the need to reign them in a bit, anyway! When the volume control on the little voices seems to be broken and their springs seem too tightly wound, parents get a little edgy, and that was happening to one of my friends.

Tim is the proud father of three excitable little girls, two of whom were expressing their zest for life at our picnic. While we were eating, everything was somewhat under control. As we were finishing and looking forward to some time of fellowship, however, the youngsters got more restless. It is a difficult thing for little ones to sit still because they are trying to see and experience all that they can; they're growing, and there sometimes aren't enough hours in the day! I could tell that their boisterous play was bothering Tim more than anyone else, so I looked for some help to settle the situation. And like a tiny angel, a cute little ladybug landed on the picnic table. With a great deal of care, I placed my finger in front of it and—sure enough—it crawled onto my hand. I called the two girls over to our table and proceeded to show them my sweet little friend. After

cautioning them to handle the tiny creature with care, I placed it in their hands. The change that took place was instantaneous! Both of them went over to the foot of a tree and sat down. They talked to the ladybug and studied it as it took the longest walk of its small life.

Bugs seem to have a certain affect on kids, don't they? Children can watch ants scurrying about doing their daily chores, or study a beetle trying to make its way through the jungle of a lawn for destinations unknown! As a small boy, the other kids my age and I would take glass jars, poke holes in the lids with an old nail, place some carefully plucked flowers in it and deftly catch a couple of bees to look at for a while. As I reminisce on that time, I hope the trauma wasn't too great on those poor little creatures!

But of all the insects that exist, there is a group that stands (or should I say *flies*) above the rest like some royal family! Butterflies and moths are in a class by themselves! When I was young, all I wanted to do was look at them: no capturing, no touching, just staring in wonder! I'm still that way! They seem to be priceless gems and so delicate that, if touched, they would dissolve before one's very eyes. Looks can be deceiving, however! Some butterflies are so strong they can migrate—like birds—thousands of miles. Others have been known to survive attacks by birds and other predators a little worse for wear but alive nonetheless. With approximately 17,000 species worldwide and 700 in North America, there is a very good chance that all of us can see some extraordinary happenings in these creatures' lives. One may see an aggressive Mourning Cloak or a Red Admiral chasing a bird out of its territory! It may be possible for you to see a bird or animal choke and gag after trying to eat a Monarch: their colours are actually a warning to all predators that they are inedible (a by-product of the milkweed plant their caterpillars feed on). Some, like the Buckeye, will "pop" their wings open when a bird approaches them; a couple of large eyes are revealed on their wings, which is often enough to frighten away all sorts of predators. But, although these are amazing things, the greatest of all wonders in the butterfly realm is seen in their growth from stage to stage.

In ancient times, butterflies and caterpillars were considered two separate insects. When you look at them, you certainly can't blame the ancients for thinking that way, can you? The only other change of that extent in nature exists in frogs (from tadpoles to adult frogs)! However, it is this transformation—the slow, earthbound worm to the angelic, glittering marvel—that we shall think about here. Caterpillars grow at an alarming rate. In two to four weeks it will have gone from a miniature hatchling to a pupa or chrysalis, shedding its skin four to six times in the process. It literally eats 'till it bursts! In the chrysalis, the pudgy, sluggish herbivore develops wings and adult organs through hormonal changes over a two-week period. As it emerges from the hardened case that surrounded it, the newly formed insect gulps air to make its wings expand and harden. In a matter of hours, it is earth-bound no longer!

Did you know that this type of change can happen to human beings too? Let's have a look. The Bible places all people in one of two different categories. Sure, there are male and female, Jews and Gentiles, saints and sinners, Christians and non-Christians, but there is another set of classifications in Scripture. From a strictly spiritual context, there are two types of people walking this earth: conformed people and transformed people.

In Romans 12:1-2, Paul defines this for us:

> *Therefore, I urge you, brothers, in view of God's mercy, to offer your bodies as living sacrifices, holy and pleasing to God—this is your spiritual act of worship. Do not conform any longer to the pattern of this world, but be transformed by the renewing of your mind. Then you will be able to test and approve what God's will is—his good, pleasing and perfect will.*

In this passage, the apostle throws a caution at believers. He uses this caution to assess the direction of Christian lives. They are either different because of a special divine influence or they are, simply, adopting the low standards of a secular, carnal society. To best comprehend this disparity, we will have to check out the two terms "conformed" and "transformed."

Conformed

There are three elements in the concept "conformed:" deform, reform and conform. Deformity of the human race (or sin) started not long after man and woman was formed (or created). *"Sin entered the world through one man, and death through sin, and in this way death came to all men..."* (Rom. 5:12). We inherited a sin nature and have been tainted by Adam's disobedience; it's in our genes and there's no escaping it! However, we add to the problem by sinning ourselves: *"...for all have sinned and fall short of the glory of God"* (Rom. 3:23). This truth is obvious to all. To deny it is to deny one's self! However, we go further than this by not only practicing sin but by approving it as well (Rom. 1:32). This is conformity! Eve presented us with this element of sin in the garden of Eden. She ate of the forbidden fruit and then prompted Adam to partake of it, also. Mankind is powerless to stop this plague; so much of our time is spent trying to lighten our load by redefining sin and eliminating guilt. This does nothing, of course, to meet the real need. C.S. Lewis once wrote what we all know to be true:

> For the first time I examined myself with a serious practical purpose. And there I found what appalled me: a zoo of lusts, a bedlam of ambitions, a nursery of fear, a harem of fondled hatreds. My name was Legion.[1]

And lest we think it is only the spiritually inclined who think thus, note the terse condemnation that flowed from the pen of H.G. Wells: "Man was created for an empire but is living in a pit."[2] The misnomer of this century, however, came from Christian lips (of all places): there is absolutely no biblical support for anything as fatuous as "the moral majority"! The greatest portion of earth's population is conformist! People do what others want them to do, and they even do what they *think* others want them to do. Even the element of reform is conformity. Religious people delude themselves with the idea that being good-natured and being "good" on an elementary level will alleviate the problem of not living up to the impermeable law of God. Hoping to produce a change on the inside (the heart and soul of a person), they attempt to perform religious duties and activities on the outside (Jesus called such things "white-washed tombs" in Matthew 23:27).

When we conform to the pattern of this world (even religiously) we think we are being adaptable, individualistic and even open-minded. The truth, however, comes from the Word of God:

> *...you were dead in your transgressions and sins, in which you used to live when you followed the ways of this world and of the ruler of the kingdom of the air, the spirit who is now at work in those who are disobedient. All of us also lived among them at one time, gratifying the cravings of our sinful natures and following its desires and thoughts. Like the rest, we were by nature objects of wrath (Eph. 2:1-3).*

We *know* this to be true, don't we? It is beyond question and beyond debate; we are without excuse! But there is another kind of life than this hopelessness.

Conformity is not just doing what the world does, it is thinking the way the world thinks. Romans 12:1-2 was written to Christians. They are the ones who ought to be setting the standards by which we live. Too often, however, believers must come to this portion of Scripture and reacquaint themselves with what God wants: a people set apart for Himself, a people that leaves the influence of a sinful world behind, a people desirous of God's will and not their own.

Transformed

In Romans 12:1-2, the word used to express this divine change in a person is the Greek word, *metamorphoo*. It sounds amazingly familiar, doesn't it? Metamorphosis is the total change we see in many insects and several amphibians. Many things, however, go through metamorphosis (complete, unequivocal change into another form). The food we eat is transformed into energy by digestion. Water changes into ice or steam through temperature adjustment. Minerals turn into metals by subjecting them to intense heat. Wood becomes furniture through the skills of a carpenter. Clay turns into pottery at the hands of a potter. In all these cases, and many more, the metamorphosis is caused by an external force at work; such vast change is not

possible by the effort, determination or will of the object being altered. And man cannot transform himself anymore than these items. There may be some miniscule things each person can refashion in themselves, but the basic makeup of mankind can never be tampered with by the effort, determination or will of man.

The basic makeup I have mentioned here defines the parameters of transformation in us. There are six basic states within each human being on this planet: physical, mental, social, emotional, psychological and spiritual. Four of these (physical, mental, social and emotional) are relatively equal in all men. There are variations and anomalies within this layout but none so great as to remove anyone from equality status with others. When we compare ourselves to God, we are all the same regardless of what level we envision humanity on. The amount of change we can conduct within these elements is minimal. The psychological element of each human being is quite dependent upon the balance of the first four states of mankind; thus, it, too, is subject to only a little degree of change. These five dispositions are primarily under the influence of man. We can make alterations to ourselves but only within the boundaries dictated by the limitations of humanity.

The last phase or element of mankind (spirit) is completely beyond man's control. Our spiritual health and destiny is something we cannot attain through our own efforts. No individual is capable of earning a place in heaven, no person is capable of saving his or her own soul, no person can prevent the dominance of sin in life. And no one can be transformed at all unless that transformation happens spiritually. What a quandary to be in! But we see in Scripture that God is the one who transforms. He does this through the saving sacrifice of Jesus Christ: when Jesus took my sins upon Himself and died upon the cross, He allowed me—and every other person who ever lived—the chance to be freed from the penalty of sin.

Look at what a transformed person is. First of all, being transformed by the grace of God removes the weight of the law from every believer! It is displaced through God's compassion and a person's faith. The fulfillment of the law has been accomplished by Jesus Christ, and now it is drawn *through* a Christian's life to serve God (Eph. 2:10) but not as a prerequisite for salvation. Our motivation for serving God is love, not the law (1 John 4:19). The object of our service is Christ, not the law (Phil. 1:21). Our guide to serving God is the Holy Spirit, not the law (Gal. 5:16-18). As someone once, fittingly, stated, "The law can pursue a man to Calvary, but no farther!"

Secondly, transformation affects our minds and hearts; that's what Romans 12:1-2 is all about. This describes a total renovation of attitude and thought. We are not only able to control our thought life through the power of Christ (2 Cor. 10:5), we are able to actually own the same mind-set Jesus had—that of a divine servant (Phil. 2:5) and to understand the deeper spiritual perspectives of God's plan for the world and ourselves (1 Cor. 2:16)! With this kind of mind, one will not fall prey to *"hollow and deceptive"* philosophies that trap so many others (Col. 2:8).

Thirdly, transformation gives us responsibility and purpose. A Christian has been given the power to "walk" (live) as Jesus did (1 John 2:6 and 1 Pet. 2:21). Not only is the Son of God our Saviour, He is also our life, our model and our example. And we follow Him by picking up our crosses daily (Matt. 16:24). If ever there was something termed the "highest calling" of mankind, this is it!

Fourthly, transformation changes the way we see things (2 Cor. 5:16; 2 Cor. 3:16-18). After I came to Christ for salvation, I was astonished to find that, when I looked back on my life without Him, it all appeared to be like a mass of shadows. As I scan my memory and think of past activities, everything I did and was involved in is a dark image in my mind. It truly does feel like I have come to the light! I do not view people as I once did; they are no longer just entities and characters that drift in and out of my schedule for my benefit. They are eternal relationships that have a bearing upon my life while I, in turn, have a bearing upon theirs. We are all linked with eternal bands that interact for the greater glory of God throughout time itself! A Christian looks beyond the material world when he or she has been transformed. Things have a deeper meaning and a richer existence!

A spiritually transformed life, when contrasted with a worldly conformed life, is as devastatingly different on an eternal plane as the vast difference between the caterpillar and the butterfly! May it be that we not only know the difference but experience it as well. What a wonderful world this would be if there were more butterflies in it!

Chapter Twelve

During one winter's-day walk several years ago, my parents were startled and surprised to find a large, immaculately-white owl fearlessly staring at them from its perch ten feet off the ground in the Gillies Lake forest. A daytime sighting of any owl is rare, but seeing a resident of Arctic regions in our forests is a once-in-a-lifetime opportunity!

When winter in the Arctic is particularly bad and the cycle of lemming populations are at their lowest ebb, we—in northern Ontario—are sometimes blessed with the presence of a visitor from the far north. These great birds have even been recorded and seen in northern states like Minnesota and Michigan. The Snowy Owl prefers its own frigid habitat and its own diet, but, during difficult years, it will head south to climes where *any* prey can be found. Even though it relies heavily upon the lemming of the tundra, it will dine on rabbits, birds, rodents, mice and other small animals of the boreal forest.

In the dense forests of northern Ontario, the Snowy Owl becomes quite conspicuous but, because of its extraordinary physical characteristics, this does not hinder its hunting ability. Of all the owls of the world, it is the heaviest at 70 ounces; although it is not the tallest. In order to function and survive in the Arctic, it requires body mass. The greater the mass of a creature, the less heat-loss endured! To augment its structure, the Snowy Owl is also completely covered in the richest of feathered down. With only its eyes, beak and talons exposed, it can maintain a

body temperature of forty degrees Celsius in an atmospheric temperature of minus fifty degrees Celsius! While icy winds are howling all around, this owl is as comfortable as you are in your own living room!

To assist them during the hunt, owls have soft-edged flight feathers. Instead of broadcasting their approach with the whistling wings of hawks, falcons and other avian predators, they can fly in absolute silence. Prey has little chance of escape when an owl swoops in from behind. Before they even realize they are being selected as a meal, large claws and a stunning jolt administer instantaneous death.

When one thinks of an owl, however, the first thing that comes to mind is its remarkable face! Looking more like cats than birds, owls possess binocular vision like that of human beings and other earth-bound predators. It's eyes are exceptionally large in proportion to its head and, due to the number of light receptors or rods on the retina, they are four or five times more sensitive than those of any human. Unlike humans and other animals, however, the eyes of an owl are fixed and immovable in their sockets. To compensate for this, all owls have extremely flexible necks able to turn their heads a full 180 degrees horizontally (and even vertically). When such attributes are combined with their preference for nocturnal activity, it is no wonder primitive tribes often looked upon these birds with awe and fear!

Surprisingly enough, an owl's effectiveness in the dark is not due to its eyesight alone! Only by combining sight with its exaggerated sense of hearing can it navigate the darkest night. With a facial disc similar to the finest parabolic microphone, sound is funnelled into its ears, and because these ears are in a staggered position on the skull, owls hear in stereo. When a rustling occurs on the forest floor, an owl will adjust the angle of its head several times to determine the exact location of the source before it goes into a power-dive from its perch.

Most of the owl family members are nocturnal but, due to its geographical location, the Snowy Owl can be active both in broad daylight and the depths of night. During half of the Arctic year, the sun never rises; during the other half, it never sets! Watching and listening take on a whole new meaning under such circumstances!

Oddly enough, watching, waiting and listening are key elements of a believer's life too. All Christians—from the first century AD until now—have been encouraged to look for our Lord's return to this earth. Each generation of believers has watched and waited for His sudden appearance, and each generation has found comfort in the thought that Jesus could come back at any moment. This comfort or encouragement is exactly what the apostle Paul envisioned for the Church (1 Thess. 4:18) when he passed on the truth about Jesus' second coming. And theologians like Augustine saw the essence of that comfort: "He who loves the coming of the Lord is not he who affirms it is far off, nor is it he who says it is near. It is he who, whether it be far or near, awaits it with sincere faith, steadfast hope and fervent love."[1] This is the watching and waiting the Lord expects!

Over the last thirty years, we have seen a surge of eschatological interest in the Christian community with the publication of Hal Lindsay's books in the '70s, a decline in fervor after 1984 and, in the late '90s, a renewed interest in apocalyptic themes by Hollywood brought about by the Y2K problem, by potential interstellar calamities and by the significance of the year 2000. While the world may have a few reasons to reconsider the potential for planetary catastrophe, believers should be honing in on the very real possibility of our Lord's return within our lifetimes!

My friend, Ken Wood, and I sat talking about this very thing once, after a Sunday evening service. We were both excited about living in a time like this where there seems to be no more prophecies left to fulfill—in accordance with God's Word—before Christ comes back to take us home. Like two schoolboys, we felt elation at the thought! But since then, I have been looking to see if there is, indeed, nothing standing between us and that glorious day, and I have found that there may be something yet to happen. It is not mentioned very often but it is in Scripture nonetheless. If you are looking for our Lord to return anytime soon, there is something to watch out for. Paul's second epistle to the Thessalonian church tells us about it:

Concerning the coming of our Lord Jesus Christ and our being gathered to him, we ask you, brothers, not to become easily unsettled or alarmed by some prophecy, report or letter supposed to have come from us, saying that the day of the Lord has already come. Don't let anyone deceive you in any way, for

that day will not come until the rebellion occurs and the man of lawlessness is revealed, the man doomed to destruction. He will oppose and will exalt himself over everything that is called God or is worshiped, so that he sets himself up in God's temple, proclaiming himself to be God. Don't you remember that when I was with you I used to tell you these things? And now you know what is holding him back, so that he may be revealed at the proper time. For the secret power of lawlessness is already at work; but the one who now holds it back will continue to do so till he is taken out of the way. And then the lawless one will be revealed, whom the Lord Jesus will overthrow with the breath of his mouth and destroy by the splendor of his coming. The coming of the lawless one will be in accordance with the work of Satan displayed in all kinds of counterfeit miracles, signs and wonders, and in every sort of evil that deceives those who are perishing. They perish because they refused to love the truth and so be saved. For this reason God sends them a powerful delusion so that they will believe the lie and so that all will be condemned who have not believed the truth but have delighted in wickedness (2 Thess. 2: 1-12).

In the RSV, the phrase I have singled-out reads like this: *"unless the rebellion comes first."* In Matthew chapter 24 and Mark chapter 13, Jesus said to "watch" for His return and to be discerning the signs of the times. This "rebellion" is something to watch out for! The rebellion spoken of deals with Christians and those who have known the truth. In some translations, it is called a "falling away," and the original Greek word *apostasia* means "defection from the truth." One would have to know the truth or know of the truth in order to "defect" from it. Thus, we are faced with the horrible postulate that there are people within evangelical ranks who will shun faith in Christ for something else. There are a lot of substitutions out there; some of them even appear "Christian." With words that sound similar to those of Christianity, there have arisen groups who claim to have found the long-lost, secret ingredient to true spirituality. When these groups have won over believers who are already functioning and participating in an evangelical church, it isn't long before divisions start to appear in those churches. Splits and factions take place. Be careful! Don't be found running after groups that promote such things!

The "New Age" movement is infiltrating Christian circles. Its primary purpose is to water down and distort the truth. This ideology is easily detected when it is compared to Scripture, thereby revealing its unholy adherence to mysticism, folklore and dubious practices. When you hear acquaintances telling you to forget about the Word of God, to quit being a legalist (one who reveres the authority of the Bible) or that you should be holding personal revelation above specific revelation (the Bible), be on your guard! The New Age movement has found its way to you!

This is happening in our time and many are being affected. At no time does Paul say this will be a little event. It is big and it is attacking the Church as never before! Christians are being told there must be more to one's Christianity than faith in Jesus Christ. It is the old "add-on" philosophy of the Galatian church, part of the "delusion" Paul warns about. It is done with spiritual words and designed to please the flesh as it drives a wedge into the body of Christ!

There are bona fide works of the Lord happening throughout Christianity today. Miracles are not extinct. The power of God is available to all. But spiritual discernment based upon a solid knowledge of the Word of God is to be exercised in these last days because the delusion is going to be great. Remember that not all special effects are from God (Matt. 7:15-20), not all self-denying programs are instituted by our Lord (Col. 2:20-23) and special status based upon visions is not necessarily spiritual or scripturally sound (Col. 2:17-19). If there is one thing we need above all else in our day, it is the ability to discern, discern, discern (Matt. 16:3; Luke 12:56; 1John 4:1). That ability to distinguish comes from a maturity grounded not in hype, feeling, song or ecstasy but in the Word of God (Heb. 5:12-14; Heb. 4:12-13).

Although there are things to watch out for, the most imperative element of Christian living is to watch for Jesus Christ's return to this earth. Almost 2000 years have passed since our Lord cautioned us to watch (particularly in Mark 13:32-37) for His return. Christians are still watching. This has certainly given scoffers the opportunity to mock about the Lord's return. However, a cruel joke is not being perpetrated by the Lord in this instance; He is, in fact, looking for disciples, and only a true disciple is going to live like the good servants who both work and watch! It doesn't matter when our Saviour returns! All that truly matters is that we watch and serve. The apostle Paul shows he understood the Lord to mean this when he wrote Titus 2:11-14:

> *For the grace of God has appeared for the salvation of all men, training us to renounce irreligion and worldly passions, and to live sober, upright, and godly lives in this world, awaiting our blessed hope, the appearing of the glory of our great God and Saviour Jesus Christ, who gave himself for us to redeem us and to purify for himself a people of his own who are zealous for good deeds* (RSV).

The two most important events in history other than the creation of history itself are the crucifixion of the Son of God and the return of the Son of God to this earth. And just as Jesus Christ cautioned His disciples in the garden of Gethsemane, He cautions us at the end of the twentieth century: *"Watch and pray that you may not enter into temptation"* (Matt. 26:41; Mark 14:38; Luke 22:46). The command is the same—*"watch and pray."* The danger is the same—*"that you may not enter into temptation."* The disciples' temptation was to fall away and scatter when the authorities came to take Jesus away, and they failed! Our temptation is to fall away and scatter. What will we do? Even our beloved Saviour left us with the rhetorical question only we can answer: *"Nevertheless, when the Son of man comes, will He find faith on earth"* (Luke 18:8 KJV)?

By watching—expectantly—for the Lord to return at any moment, a Christian can encourage others (1 Thess. 4:18) and purify him or herself (1 John 3:3). All the blessings and benefits that stem from this vigilance are directly dependent upon the Object of our attention. No amount of watching will do us any good whatsoever unless the One we are looking for is purity personified and the Comforter of all the afflicted! We have a Blessed Hope; we have an inheritance with the saints who have gone before; we have a job to do while we wait; we are to have an ear open to hear the trumpet call and an eye watching the heavens for a glorious appearance! *"Amen. Come, Lord Jesus"* (Rev. 22:20).

Chapter Thirteen Psalm 19:1-4

As an artist, I find the limitless facades of water absolutely riveting! From the varieties of wave action to the unending vistas of sunlight reflecting from the surface of lakes and streams, the incredible beauty of watery landscapes provide joy, peace, inspiration, awe and comfort. Never has something so impersonal provided so many deep and profound feelings in mankind throughout the ages!

While producing my brushed charcoal painting known as "Canadian Reflection," I learned of the tremendous "drawing power" (no pun intended) water can have on an artist! I was truly fascinated by the Canada Goose when I started to do the layout of this piece, but scant hours later I was so enraptured with the flow of the simple waves surrounding the creature, I could have left the bird out of the picture and been totally satisfied! One can almost see character and life in its appearance and movements, and, I suppose, that is why ancient mariners (and a few modern day ones) felt they had a special relationship with the sea. It is more than just a substance; it is more than just a medium upon which watercraft float or in which humans find refreshment; it is more than scenery; it is more than a quenching of thirst; it is more than mere chemistry!

After preparing a sermon on the spiritual implications of water, the Lord confirmed the necessity of this topic with a number of incidents, including a news story on the CBC television network. Some high-profile literary awards had been handed out that very week, and the winner

of the non-fiction category was an individual who wrote a book called *Water*! There were also two chemical spills at that time: one in Russia and one in northern Ontario, a scant seventy miles north of my home. Rivers and water tables were ruined and people learned of how fragile they are without water. You can call it coincidence if you like, but I know a God who can utilize any and every situation on earth to suit His purposes, and that obliterates coincidence! He didn't have these things happen so I could backup a sermon; they happened while He drove my mind and heart into this topic. His timing is impeccable and completely beyond comprehension!

Let me share some of the extraordinary physical and spiritual facts about water. Did you know that 70 percent of our bodies are made up of water? Or that more than half of the plants and animals on earth live in the water? Or that most of our food is made up of water: tomatoes – 95 percent; spinach – 91percent; apples – 85 percent; potatoes – 80 percent; beef – 61 percent; hot dogs – 56 percent. Or that three quarters of the world is covered with water? I live in one of the most privileged countries on earth because it abounds with a vast supply of fresh water. Now stop and consider the implications and the responsibilities Canada has while reading this next fact: over *1.25 billion* people on earth have no access to a source of fresh water and, every eight seconds, a child dies because of drinking contaminated water! We have yet to grasp the importance of this substance we take for granted in North America!

I want to do more than trigger your global conscience, as important as that may be! Water has certain properties that tell us a great deal about spiritual things, and some of those things are well-known. Water exists in three states: liquid, solid and gas (a trinity).Water is also—and I want you to remember this—*never out of context*: it freezes at a specific temperature and it boils at a specific temperature.

Now when you turn to the Bible you will find God refers to the Word of God as "water" in many places (John 3:5; 1 John 5:6-12; 2 Pet. 3:1-7; Jer. 2:13; Zech. 9:11; Isa. 58:11). In many other portions of Scripture, this symbolism is implied as well, but there is one particularly delightful reference to this truth that is incredibly profound:

Husbands, love your wives, as Christ loved the church and gave himself up for her, that he might sanctify her, having cleansed her **by the washing of water with the word**, *that he might present the church to himself in splendor, without spot or wrinkle or any such thing, that she might be holy and without blemish* (Eph. 5:25-27 RSV).

In the midst of a passage that reveals the appropriate love of one spouse for another, God shares a remarkable thing with us: He points out what He is actually doing with the divinely-breathed Scriptures He gave to mankind. His intention is to cleanse the Church (universal) with Scripture! The destiny of the Church is to be a spotless bride and it says here that the Word of God makes the Church spotless. There is no suggestion or hint that any other activity will do that job, so, if there is not a total commitment on our part to place ourselves under the authority of Scripture, we simply won't be *"holy and without blemish."*

The substance that we call water can be appreciated by each one of us in three basic ways: 1) I've looked at lakes, ponds and streams all over this wonderful country. There have been beautiful sights logged into my memory and some that are rather repulsive, too. When one appreciates a watery scene, it is usually because the water itself reflects some of its surroundings—it acts like a mirror. But if I were to simply look at water—as in a glass—there is seldom anything spectacular to see. In fact, I would see nothing but the glass or what lies on the other side of the glass. Scripture is like that, too. If you just look at it and read it, you may see nothing special. After all, it's just another book to some people, words on a page.

2) When I take a shower in the morning, I do more than look at the water coming out of the nozzle. I let the water flow over my body and use it to clean myself before setting out for the day. I'm experiencing something more than a mere impression; the water is actually doing something for me and to me. Scripture is like that, too. If you study it, it will touch your life. Its power will rise off the printed page and begin to affect your life.

3) My body requires a certain amount of water every day, or it will dehydrate. By taking a glass of water and drinking it, I am doing more than touching it or having it touch me. When I drink

water, it becomes a part of me. Scripture is like that, too. When you memorize it—not just for the sake of memory but for the sake of utilizing it—it becomes a part of you. Its living reality meets your living reality and fashions a new kind of person based upon the redemption that has been birthed in you by the Son of God and nurtured in you by the Holy Spirit.

In John 7:37-39, Jesus stood up in the midst of a crowd when the High Priest was pouring a water-offering beside the altar of the temple. This ceremony was performed on the last day of the Feast of Tabernacles—"the great day." It was the great day because it declared to every Jew that God would provide when faith in Him was exercised: sacrifice this water to Him—as a type of "firstfruits"—before the rainy season begins, and He will take care of you! So Jesus took this opportunity to declare that only in Him could a life of unparalleled spiritual beauty and spiritual provision be sustained. When He said that *"out of* (a believer's) *heart shall flow rivers of living water"* (v. 38), He was referring to the Holy Spirit which was yet to come. When we want to know what this overflow of living water is like, we need only turn to the Word of God to find out. In Galatians 5:22, we are told what the fruits of the Holy Spirit are, and, amazingly enough, each one of these (love, joy, peace, patience, kindness, goodness, faithfulness, gentleness, self-control) is an internal state of being! These things flow out of a believer when the Holy Spirit does His job of revealing truth and glorifying Christ (John 14:15-21; John 16:5-15). Now, here's the key: only the God-breathed Scriptures can make this happen in you. You can search for the Holy Spirit of God anywhere you want, but there is only one place where you are *guaranteed* of finding 100 percent of Him, 100 percent of the time, and that is within the pages of your Bible! If we are overflowing with the living water Jesus proclaimed that day, we shall be overflowing with the Word of God. I once heard C.H. Spurgeon quoted as he commented about the spiritual beauty of John Bunyan, the author of *Pilgrim's Progress*: "His very blood was Bibline... cut him anywhere and the Word of God would flow out."

In our day, we need more Biblicists, not fewer. We have enough *"waterless springs"* (2 Pet. 2:17) roaming around the country. Jude calls them *"waterless clouds"* (Jude 12). These teachers are waterless because they do not have the Holy Spirit of God and they do not stand on the Word of God. What's more, they are waterless when they use the Word of God out of context (remember that phrase?). Like a person trying to make ice at 200 degrees Celsius or steam at fifty degrees below zero, they are completely off track! Promising freedom, they can only deliver slavery. History has had its full share of such people, but there seems to be a tremendous increase of them in our day!

In 2 Timothy 4:1-5, the apostle Paul cautions all generations of believers to be wary of the teachings that seem to please the palate. In this passage, condemnation is pronounced upon the hearers and seekers of "waterless spring" theology. These are people who do not wish to submit to what they *know* to be true from the Word of God. Instead, they seek after those things they *want* to be true. The Holy Spirit warns, however, that the longer this attitude prevails in a person, the more dangerous the situation becomes. There will come a point at which the wayward individual can no longer tolerate the truth. Like junk-food addicts, the mere thought of real food will "turn them off"! What often pleases the senses, provides no true nutritional value whatsoever (in spiritual as well as physical realms).

To summarize what our approach ought to be when we consider the worth of the water of the Word, turn to chapter 24 of Luke's gospel. In verses 25 to 27, our Lord Jesus shows that all Scripture has the primary purpose of teaching us about Him. To deny the Bible and its proper place in a believer's life is to actually deny the Lordship and work of Christ. In verse 32, we see that the result of searching the Scriptures is a deep, burning desire to know our Saviour more. The Bible does not stifle the work of God in you, it enhances it! In verses 44 to 48, Jesus also teaches how important our minds are. Those who have attacked the Bible lately have come from within; they maintain that the heart is more important than the mind, so one can let emotions dictate and forget about Scripture. We find, however, that Jesus does not condone such thoughts. Your mind is of the utmost importance to Him. He is looking for disciples who will allow Him to transform their minds by a holy focus upon the holy Scriptures. This is not a worship of the Book but rather a worship of the Lord by means of the Book He has graciously provided.

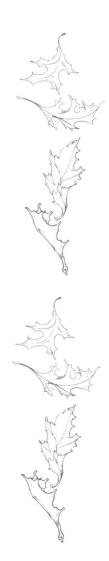

The thirst you may be experiencing right now is likely a result of avoiding the Word of God. Your spirit, soul and mind were fashioned to find life within the revelation God has given. Refresh yourself. Drink of the water of the Word. Let it wash you and fill you, and dehydrate yourself no longer!

Chapter Fourteen PSALM 19:1-4

A little more than a year ago, I hopped into my car and headed out from home on a very early summer morning. The sun was just on the rise, and there was a beautiful calm about the forest that surrounds my house. The main highway—completely free of all traffic—wound like a wide, wet pathway up and over the hill before me. As I accelerated up this small hill, I noticed a familiar sight. Thousands of motorists see this every day, and yet, this special morning I was going to learn from an experience that I, and many others, had taken for granted for years.

At the top of the hill there was a large crow feeding on something in the middle of the road. A "road kill" from the night before had caught his attention. I was approximately 200 meters away when I spotted him, but I was closing the gap between us rapidly. When I got to within twenty meters of the crow and his breakfast, the bird hopped nonchalantly over the dual yellow lines of the highway and waited for my car to pass. Being only an arm's length from my roaring vehicle, he reminded me of a little matador dodging a bull the size of a house! I slowed down a little so I could watch the crow in my rearview mirror. And, right on cue, he hopped back over the lines to continue with his repast.

Now, that may not seem like anything extraordinary to you, but let me explain what happened: that crow and thousands more like him all over the country, are learning things from you and I. What I saw was not some instinctive reaction that lies within the bird. This manoeuvre was learned behavior! His natural urge would be to fly away in fright. And I dare say that, if you were his size and my car was approaching you at eighty kilometers per hour, you'd fly away in fright, too! But the crow fought that urge and stayed on the highway because he learned that the huge, lethal, metal automobiles that race up and down this path, stay on the right side. It would have been an easy thing to simply swerve the car and run over this little guy; many have done that in total ignorance of the wonderful spectacle that was represented before them.

The crow family (*corvidae*) is an amazing branch of the North American songbird population. They are the largest of the songbirds (without much musical talent!) which includes ravens, magpies, nutcrackers and jays. Among the most intelligent of the animal kingdom, they are capable of mimicking other creatures, of using tools and of problem solving. All of the family members of *corvidae* are called bold by most people. They tend to push smaller birds around, rob nests on occasion and their colours are striking in many instances. But the real reason for them being described as bold is their irritable call.

When we think of boldness in our day, we often perceive it with negative connotations: the spoiled brat that used to visit our house (and turn it upside down), the audacious teenager that thought the world revolved around him, the arrogant young gal with the good looks and the sharp tongue. We've all encountered these before, haven't we? The Bible, however, doesn't see boldness in that way. In Acts 4:13, we are told of the boldness of Peter and John before the sanhedrin: *"Now when they saw the boldness of Peter and John, and perceived that they were uneducated, common men, they wondered; and they recognized that they had been with Jesus"* (RSV). These apostles stood up and testified to the saving power of Jesus Christ when all the authorities opposed them. They had absolute confidence in the truth of the matter.

We are also told, in the Word of God, that we can now enter the sanctuary of God in heaven with "confidence" because of the blood of Christ (Heb. 10:19). There is no pride here! There is only a living out of the truth set before us: Jesus is my Saviour; heaven is my home; I am a child of God; I can count on seeing my Father when I need to; I should be doing what He wants of me!

My position in Christ is designed to have an effect on my practice: I do not spend all of my time and energy on simply examining and cross-examining my status as a Christian. I should have the assurance that I can put truth into practice! Such boldness is a good thing.

If there is no standing out *for* our faith and no standing out *with* our faith, where is our "city" and our "light" (Matt. 5:14-15)? These weren't passive expectations of the Son of God; He is looking for results! He is looking for faith lived out! There is supposed to be some affirmative action here! Not long ago, I came across an admonition that was delivered by David Fuller, and it bears repeating: "If you were arrested for being a Christian, would there be enough evidence to convict you?"[1] Certainly, Peter and John lived up to that. Can you and I?

In North America, bold persons are those who get angry and impatient on the highways and byways, those who shout at you and attack you at children's sporting events, those who push their way to the front of the line instead of waiting their turn, those who park in handicapped zones in violation of the law, those who demand their rights at the expense of others' rights. And yet, North America is a land of incredible compromise where complacency and uninvolvement are the true components behind the politically-correct term we know as "tolerance." A true boldness—a Scriptural boldness—is desperately needed in our time. When the apostle John wrote *"Little children let us not love in word or speech but in deed and in truth"* (1 John 3:18), the Holy Spirit is telling us we ought to stand up and step out in faith. A disciple is bold, not for himself, but always for His Lord. Opportunities abound in this western culture of ours. It should be easy to shine for Jesus here because the darkness is so great. And if we are not responding now, what will we be doing when things get worse?

Do you make a difference in your community, or does your community make the difference in you? "The only thing necessary for the triumph of evil is for good men to do nothing."[2]

©R M Smith

Chapter Fifteen Psalm 19:1-4

There are two incidents in my life that rank among my clearest memories. One took place approximately thirty-four years ago, and the other took place in 1997. One happened at night, the other during the day; one while in a tent, the other in a car; one in the summer, the other in the winter. They both involved an encounter with a legendary creature.

Shuman Lake is located in the backwoods of Cobalt, three or four miles out the Hound Chutes Road and approximately one mile off that road. It is an isolated and treacherous place—exactly where five or six teenage boys would like to spend the weekend! Most of us were quite familiar with the bush, so there was extremely little for our parents to worry about.

The lake is about a mile in length, and there is a small-stream outlet on the south end. We pitched our tent halfway up the eastern shoreline. Our plans were to explore the lake the next day with the use of a raft we made that evening. When the sun had set, we built a campfire and, before too long, we had some visitors. They were either curious or disturbed by our presence, and they wanted us to be aware of theirs! Down by the stream, in the darkness, came the unmistakable sounds of a wolf pack. The howls continued for at least thirty minutes and acquired the appropriate response from us. First there was shock and a twinge of fear, followed by a sudden eagerness not to let the campfire die out! After a while, however, our bush sense took over, and we realized we were not in danger. Sleep wasn't great that night, but it was not absent. The next day unfolded as we had planned after we went down the lake to see where our visitors had stationed themselves the night before.

In the winter of 1997, my wife and I were headed south after visiting family in the north. I know Highway 11 north like the back of my hand, and, when anything is a little out of place, I'll notice. We had just come through a "rock cut" (there are a lot of them up here) about five miles south of Latchford, Ontario. There was some movement beyond the snow bank on the left hand side of the road, and although I knew the form, I was not expecting to see it here! I nudged Debbie and told her to take a good look at what was clambering over the bank and onto the shoulder of the highway. I should have stopped the car to enjoy this experience longer, but there wasn't much room to pull over. So, in passing, our mouths fell open in wonder at the sight of an arctic wolf trotting along the highway for 100 yards! This was a lone wolf, and he was far below the southern boundaries of his normal habitat, a vision I shall not soon forget!

Although they are not truly dangerous to human beings, wolves are quite lethal to natural prey and even livestock. In the past, members of the various aboriginal tribes played with wolf pups and revered the adults, but currently, in the Nipissing region, these nocturnal raiders are causing quite a commotion among local farmers. Some livestock has been lost, and the wolf is to blame. In the Bible, too, the wolf is often viewed with disdain, but that is quite understandable: what else would one expect within the pages of manuscripts from a nation whose primary livelihood consisted of raising sheep and cattle? Consequently, this does not mean the wolf is the personification of evil. It is merely contrasted with sheep so we might comprehend some specific spiritual truth.

Wolves have many positive attributes. They have an intricate social order in which one dominant couple (the "alpha" couple) act like king and queen. The pack that surrounds them is usually made up of family, and the alpha couple is the only breeding pair in camp. They live in a cooperative, where everyone knows their place and their tasks. Communication by use of body language is frequent and often quite affectionate among themselves. Their hunting tactics include relay teams that can wear out large prey like moose and deer. However, their most common food sources are smaller game like rabbits, grouse, squirrels and mice. Carrion is not beneath their notice, either!

Although they exhibit the qualities of intelligence, social order, teamwork and lifetime mating, there is one characteristic that truly stands out—their abilities as long-distance runners. They have an enormous capacity for endurance that can be applied to the Christian life. The apostle Paul was led by the Holy Spirit to write: *"I have fought the good fight, I have finished the race, I have kept the faith"* (2 Tim. 4:7 RSV), and, *"Brethren, I do not consider that I have made it my own; but one thing I do, forgetting what lies behind and straining forward to what lies ahead, I press on towards the goal for the prize of the upward call of God in Christ Jesus"* (Phil. 3:13-14 RSV).

A good runner has three principles to keep in mind when training and racing. I was a sprinter in my youth, but these guidelines apply to marathoners as well: 1) practice, practice, practice; 2) keep the finish line as your number one priority; 3) forget/deny the pain and weariness.

In practice, a runner learns techniques, fundamentals and strategies through repetition. In Christianity one must always be learning; with a limitless God, there is always something for us to learn, and that is why both Paul and we can state, *"I do not consider that I have made it…."* There are techniques and fundamentals (the "how to's") in the Christian life. And the first one is to get a good coach. The best coaches are those who have also been runners. When you seek friends and mentors, gather around yourself those who are mature and strong, those who have run and are continuing to run for the Lord. So many of the tragedies in life come from not having the right people around you. Scripture shows us the value of having someone to whom we ought to be accountable: Timothy, Silas and a host of others had Paul as their coach; Elisha had Elijah; Apollos had Aquilla and Priscilla; even Theophilus had Luke. Young Christians—and that doesn't simply mean young in natural age—look around yourselves! The need in the world is great, and the time is growing exceedingly short! See the wealth of experience represented by the "mature" brothers and sisters in Christ that surround you. Seek out a coach and then listen and learn.

When you learn the fundamentals and techniques of running, you are hammering into yourself the basics of running. It is no different in the Christian life. It takes time to learn about Christ and about yourself. It also takes effort. Sound teaching is an absolute must in the growth of a believer, so that is your "starting line."

Strategies are also important. You must apply the knowledge of the fundamentals and techniques as you run the race, and only by listening to the guidance of Jesus Christ and the Holy Spirit can this happen. You see, your coach and mentor can take you through the fundamentals and techniques, but once you're on the track he cannot run with you. Circumstances are always changing during a race, and, therefore, making the right adjustments is absolutely vital if you are to win or even finish. When you depend upon what you've learned, the Holy Spirit of God will help you to apply it. And don't get so caught up in the wonder of running you forget *why* you are running at all; your feet, your learning, your effort and your stamina are not to be your focus. Press on! To what? To the goal which is *"the prize of the upward call of God,"* none other than Jesus Christ Himself!

Hosea put it this way: *"Let us know, let us press on to know the Lord..."* (Hos. 6:3). Our goal is to know God. This is what eternal life is, according to Jesus: *"And this is eternal life, that they know thee the only true God, and Jesus Christ whom thou has sent"* (John 17:3 RSV).

In the summer of 2001, I was asked to be the keynote speaker at a central Ontario camp. My responsibility was to teach art during the afternoon and to preach to the varsity students in the evening. I like to shock people sometimes, and I had the opportunity to do so there. Based on the Word of God, I told them the main purpose of their local church was not the salvation of souls. There were quite a few open-mouthed stares directed at me, but I went on to show them why they should understand that concept: a church that focuses on that as their goal will not grow and be of use to the Lord. A church that focuses on that only will attempt to get people saved and then leave them in abject infancy. The church's real goal is that people might *know* the Lord (in personal relationship). Salvation is the vehicle by which people start to know the Lord, but it does not end there. Ephesians 4:11-16 gives us the complete mandate of the Church *and* the very reason we press on in our Christian lives. To know God is to have eternal life because He is the only source of eternal life. It is not just a matter of getting rid of our sins, it is a matter of receiving something as well.

Keeping the finish line as your number-one priority does not mean our center of attention should be heaven, our "mansion in the sky," the "pearly gates," our robes of white, the crowns we shall wear or any other reward. See what the apostles considered their finish line: Paul's life was completely wrapped up in the fact that Jesus Christ was his life and therefore his finish line (Col. 3:1-4). John's life and hope revolved around the fact that one day he would be like his Lord (1 John 3:1-3).

There is only one finish line and only one way to cross it. We don't spend our time waving at the crowd, looking for support, endorsement and fulfillment. We don't keep our eyes on the laurel wreath, the gold medal or the blue ribbon. We don't waste valuable energy and attention on imagining what great runners we happen to be. The only thing that should keep us reaching and straining toward that heavenly tape is Jesus Christ Himself.

Forgetting and denying the pain and weariness of the race is a key element in running. I can remember being the "second leg" of a 4 x 400-meter relay team in high school. My specialty was the 110-meter hurdles, so a 400-meter distance was like running a marathon! When I was still 100 meters from the finish line, it seemed like my feet were anchored in quick sand! At that point, a runner has to get beyond the pain.

In Christian circles, we are usually concerned about how much we can remember. Planting the Word of God in our minds and hearts involves memorization. Praying for missionaries, working on Bible studies, being effective in our ministry, serving others and going the extra mile requires our powers of recall. But in Philippians chapter 3, Paul's attention is upon what we can forget. Elsewhere, the writer of the book of Hebrews cautions us to lay aside the things that hold us back (Heb. 12:1). Can you deny and lay aside sin, worries, hurt feelings, distress, suffering, sor-

row and the cares of this life? These are the things that hinder our running and sometimes bring us to a complete stop!

We are called to press on. We can only do so when our lives are free from the trappings of this world and uncompromisingly united with the Son of God. Run with perseverance.

Chapter Sixteen PSALM 19:1-4

Only within the last few hundred years has the continent of Africa been opened up to the onslaught of European settlers and fortune hunters. I can only imagine how incredulous the common man of Europe might have been as he heard tales and descriptions of some of the strangest creatures to ever inhabit this planet. Think of how you might have reacted if—having never seen or heard of an elephant—you were told of a gigantic beast that stood as tall as trees with thick, wrinkled hide, a nose longer than a man is tall, ears the size of horse blankets, a call that can rival any bugle and a body weight that could crush one's front porch! Who could have ever dreamed of such a beast?

Needless to say, that is only the beginning of the truly extraordinary animals that make Africa their home. And throughout all of my life, I have had a fondness for another almost mythological creature from the "dark continent." Only by travelling to the Toronto zoo, however, could I ever get to see one, and after doing that, I am still absolutely astounded by the image and the power and beauty of it. The sight of a rhinoceros is beyond words to me!

It is the second largest land mammal on earth, with adults tipping the scales between 4,000 and 6,000-plus pounds. It is five to six feet tall at the shoulder and approximately fourteen feet in total length. The longest horn on its nose measures three to four feet in length and is used for digging up plants and roots. The thick hide drapes the animal in folds that look like armored plat-

129

ing, but one must realize that these creatures are definitely not bullet-proof! Adult males are quite solitary and reclusive, but others form small herds, particularly on the plains and grasslands. Almost human-like in their lifespan, they live to the ripe old age of forty to sixty years if they can avoid the constant threat of poachers. They have no natural enemies, and yet four out of the five rhinoceros species are nearing extinction. This is solely due to man. They are killed in order to acquire the horns which fetch high prices, particularly on the Asian market where they are valued as an aphrodisiac, the equivalent of Viagra, I suppose! While I worked for a number of years in the fur-harvesting industry, I had the displeasure of witnessing the same devastation (for the same reasons) of the Canadian Black Bear. Bear galls were more valuable than gold in the Orient, and countless bears had been killed, gutted for one organ, and the remains were left to rot or to be scavenged in the forest. It's a sad testimony to the true attitude and desire of man.

Rhinos have very poor eyesight but extremely keen senses of smell and hearing. In one of his beautiful books of wildlife art, Robert Bateman—who has long been the standard for natural realists the world over—writes:

> Once, while on safari in East Africa, we had a close call with a Rhinoceros. We had stopped our Volkswagon bus to take pictures of him as he loped steadily toward us. He wasn't charging but he kept getting closer and closer and showed no sign of swerving. Perhaps he simply hadn't seen us yet and would change course when he did. But I wasn't about to wait around and find out. Rhinos have been known to charge a vehicle and they can make mincemeat out of one. Fortunately our engine turned over on the first try and we were soon safely out of the animal's path.[1]

Some people get all the good memories, eh?

We are going to look at the most obvious trait of this creature and, in order to do that, I want you to use your imagination for just a moment. Picture yourself locked in a room, twenty-feet square, doors bolted, windows barred, room empty. Picture an adult male rhino in that room with you—nothing else, just you and him! There would be three basic things happening besides you trying to become wallpaper at the far end of the cubicle: 1) you and I would be instantly aware of the *power* of this animal even if it did nothing but stand there; 2) we'd respect and fear the beast; 3) we'd take no liberties at any time with this creature!

In Hebrews 12:18-29, we are told of Someone else who should elicit such a response from us. The writer tells us of an awesome God and of the proper response to Him. You might envision God in many different ways: a God of love and kindness; a God of grace; a God of justice; a God of truth; a God of mercy, and all of these are scripturally accurate. But there is one attribute of God that we let slip away on us too often. I suppose it is easily forgotten because there is no way for us—as humans—to relate to it. And yet, when we forget this characteristic of God, we lose sight of Who we are dealing with: our God is the Almighty, the Creator of all that is, omnipotent, supreme. When we disregard who God is, we also get confused with what He wants of us, so the writer of the book of Hebrews brings us back to this most fundamental concept by looking to the past and the future. The Israelites trembled with fear (v. 21) before God at Sinai, and we are forewarned to give God acceptable worship, with reverence and awe (v. 28). And if we need any convincing, consider this: everything is going to be "shaken." Ask anyone who has lived through a terrible earthquake, and they will tell you they were overwhelmed by a sense of complete and utter helplessness. It is the ultimate realization that you are not in control, no matter what you do!

There is nothing on earth that is unshakable. There is also nothing in the universe that's unshakable, either (v. 26)! You'd think we would have learned this lesson by now and turned to the Almighty God in order to obtain *"a kingdom that cannot be shaken"* (v. 28), but it hasn't happened. And we are, therefore, left with this terrifying picture of the future.

God is telling us that—even in this "age of grace"—we ought not forget Who is in control! And in the book of Revelation, where countless redeemed souls are honouring and praising Him, note that he is not *doing* anything in particular. God is being praised for who He is! And if we need a

portion of Scripture to tell us what God wants in worship, Hebrews 12:28-29 is it. So many are trying to worship the way *they want to* and have left *"spirit and truth"* (John 4:23) behind. But in Hebrews 12, there is no foolishness, no self-glorification and no religious experience by those who worship. There is only God and you and no playing around! You are completely consumed with the presence of God, and all games and nonsense are burned away by the consuming fire! To worship in spirit and in truth is to be unaware of yourself completely. Godly qualities are like that. Humble men don't focus upon their humility; faithful people do not center their lives around faith; worshippers do not have to work up feelings of worship. The Object of our attention should never be ourselves if the truth be told!

The Israelites of the Old Testament learned about honouring God the hard way. When they objected to doing things God's way, it wasn't too long before they learned how serious God is about such matters. If God said to slay a lamb in a certain way, no other way would do! If God said to pour out a libation offering in a specific way, no other way would do! If God wanted a special memorial festival for eight days, nine days is too long and seven days is too short! If God said that priests should come before Him only with holy fire for the burning of incense, no other fire is acceptable! In our day, there is far too little concern about God's ways. Doing what's right in our own eyes and what feels good is the standard. There is no thought of Who we are dealing with!

Hebrews chapter 12 states that the carnal mind focuses on the physical world, and we are cautioned not to let that perspective infiltrate the body of Christ. All things were created for good, but if those things interfere with our true recognition of God, He will be obliged to shake them! Nothing is to distract you from worshiping our Almighty God as He expects you to! You would never be distracted from a rhino in your room; how much more ought God to command your attention?

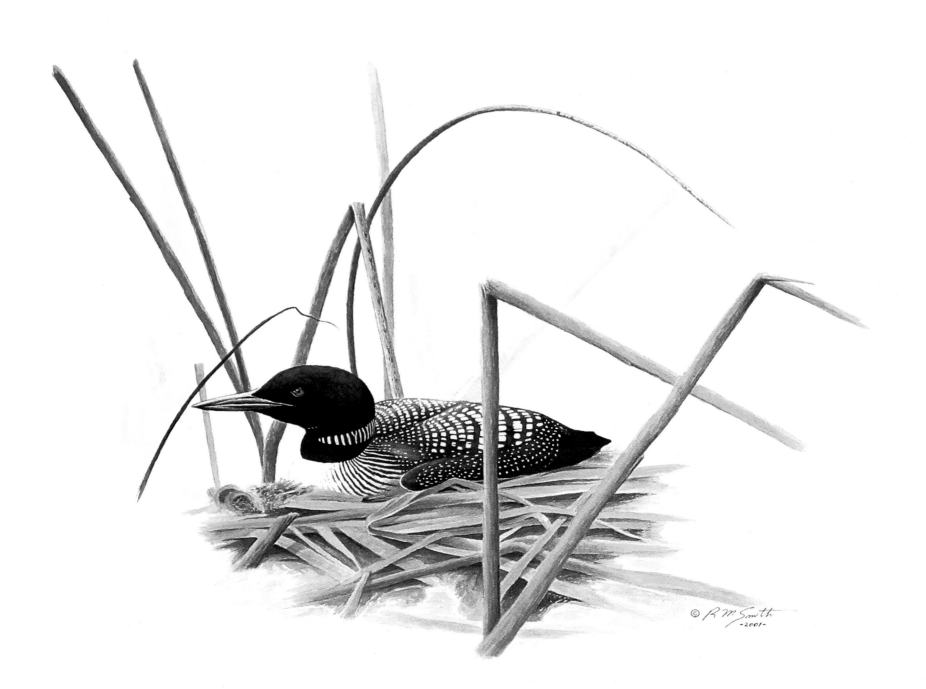

Chapter Seventeen Psalm 19:1-4

I've had some strange friends during my lifetime: jocks, acid-heads, upper-crusters, professors, drop-outs, book worms, down-and-outers, mechanics, contractors, saved, unsaved—from one end of the scale to the other. But I can honestly say, I have never had a friend like the one I had during a summer in the early '60s.

My dad and I used to do a lot of fishing on the Montreal River by a little town called Latchford, ten miles south of Cobalt. Walleye, northern pike and perch were plentiful there. Some of the best (toughest) bait in the North, however, came from Cobalt Lake. Minnows that could survive in a lake surrounded by the chemical soup of silver mine tailings *had* to be tough, and so this is where I would go to stock up on bait. As I look back on this practice, I shudder to think of the ecological ramifications of using toxic minnows in the lakes and rivers of northern Ontario. No one stopped to even consider the results as we, in ignorance, sought to enjoy the great outdoors by destroying it with our bad habits!

I had a favourite little cove on Cobalt Lake where the shiners were abundant. To catch a dozen (or more) minnows, I would secure a piece of window screen to a sturdy pole by stringing copper wire from the four corners of the screen. Within this high-tech apparatus, I'd place a soggy ball of rolled oats or white bread. The hapless minnows found this bait irresistible. One day, I had only been at my cove for a couple of minutes with my dip net in the lake, and I was staring into the dark-

ness of the water, watching and waiting for a good group of minnows. Suddenly, a flash of black and white flew through my net and scared the life out of me! As I stood there, stunned to the core, a bird popped up out of the water about fifteen feet away! It was a loon! As it sat on the surface of the water, it seemed to say, "Look in your net, chum!" Sure enough, my net was full! And, as strange as it may sound, this scenario happened a couple of times that summer. "Loonie" and I had inadvertently set up a brief symbiotic relationship where we both benefitted from the other's presence.

Up until the 1930s, people shot loons for sport. They aren't too palatable so, other than a few aboriginal tribes, no one ate them. Within the last fifty years however, there has arisen a great love affair with these unusual birds. People from all over the world have been collecting anything and all things "loony," for they have become one of the most recognizable and popular symbols of a vanishing wilderness.

As we examine this bird, we will find out why they are among the most important subjects of this book. I wish to look at two things that should strike us deeply, and the first is the call of the loon. I would guess there isn't a man, woman or child in North America that could not distinguish the call of a loon from any other voice of the wilderness. It is so "wildernessy," I have heard film makers use it in the audio background of all sorts of wild docudramas, even those set in the desert! There are four basic calls that a loon uses: the hoot, the wail, the tremolo and the yodel. Although they use their voices for many reasons, there is one thing we should note. They call out on the water and in the air frequently. They never call while on land (other than the use of a tiny hoot whisper to their mate when they need a break from the nest).

In John 10:1-5, Jesus tells us:

"Truly, truly, I say to you, he who does not enter the sheepfold by the door but climbs in by another way, that man is a thief and a robber; but he who enters by the door is the shepherd of the sheep. To him the gatekeeper opens; the sheep hear his voice, and he calls his own sheep by name and leads them out. When he has brought out all his own, he goes before them and the sheep follow him, for they know his voice. A stranger they will not follow, but they will flee from him, for they do not know the voice of strangers" (RSV).

I am certain you could pick out a loon's voice from a host of others, but can you do the same with the voice of Jesus Christ, the good Shepherd? Can you tell, instantly, whether Jesus is talking to you or whether it is a stranger? Do you think you need some special revelation to do that? Let me tell you, there already is a special revelation for that. God's ways, God's plans, God's heart and God's voice have been taken into account when He authorized the Bible. The less you know your Bible, the less you will know Christ, and that is not guesswork, my friend. Our Saviour has set the standard Himself. During His incarnation, He continually aligned His life to the authority of the Father by adhering to the authority of the Scriptures. "It is written…" was the theme of His life. With absolute integrity, it can be stated that those who have been, and are being, led astray by listening to the voices of strangers, have ignored the Word of God in one way or another. And, more often than not, the cause of such waywardness has been a lack of examining the Scriptures objectively and obediently. When we come to the Word of God, we need to hear what God says, not what we want Him to say! We need the kind of faith that comes to Him without expectations and preconceived ideas of what He is like and how He interacts with each of us. Preconceptions—no matter how fanciful—are attempts at molding God into an image *we* have made, and in Scripture that is known as idolatry. To know the Shepherd's voice, one must spend time listening to it, not drowning it out with one's own ramblings or with the clamor of this present life.

A slight caution is also due at this point: North American Christians have been blessed with so many things, and one of them is the "red letter" Bible. Do not fall into the foolish notion that only the words of Jesus Christ matter in our knowing Him and His voice. Jesus can be heard in the psalms as well as the gospels, in Exodus as well as the book of Revelation! The episode on the road to Emmaus (Luke 24:27) is proof enough for that.

The second aspect of a loon's life that is appropriate to us comes from its feet. Because the loon's feet are so far back on its body, it has tremendous power in the water and tremendous difficulty on land! It is not built for life on land! The loon finds its nourishment, its refuge, its freedom and its purpose in the water. Ninety-nine percent of its life is spent in the water. If it weren't

for the water, a loon would never be able to fly because the structure and density of its body needs a long runway with minimal surface resistance. Only on the water can a loon get its body into the proper position for take-off. For us, the meaning is clear, and the apostle John, through the Holy Spirit, states it like this:

> *Do not love the world or the things in the world. If any one loves the world, love for the Father is not in him. For all that is in the world, the lust of the flesh and the lust of the eyes and the pride of life, is not of the Father but is of the world* (1 John 2:15-16 RSV).

Let me put it simply: Christians were not redeemed for life in the world. A problem exists if a Christian feels comfortable with the world's standards, the world's attitudes, the world's perspectives, the world's expectations or the world's desires. The most awkward thing in a believer's life should be living in this world because we weren't created for that purpose. Once more, let me draw your attention to the fact that God calls His Word water in many places. And take a lesson from the loon. We can jeopardize our spiritual safety when we ignore these truths; as Christians, our nourishment is found in the water, our refuge is in the water, our freedom is in the water, our purpose is in the water and our ability to fly (worship) is possible because of the water!

Pick up a Bible. Look at it. It looks like a book, doesn't it? It has a front cover, a back cover and pages in between with writing on them. If you see only a book, you're not looking at it properly. To the natural mind, it seems like any other book. But to someone who is given new life by the Spirit of God, there is no limit to this revelation! It has no front cover and no back cover. It is a piece of eternity that has been dropped into temporal existence by the hand of God. It is a living revelation in this world of death. Each and every phrase of God's Word can remake a life because it is the power and authority of God on earth. If it weren't so important to the life of a believer, God would not have wasted the time and energy of those who wrote it, nor would He have wasted the lives of those who were martyred so we might have a copy in our hands. If you knew how it came to you, you might treat it differently!

Relish the opportunity of living in the Word of God. It is given so you might have life, spiritual health and security within the hands and heart of God. To ignore it for the sake of something else is to ignore the state of one's own soul! Jesus is our life, and He has provided us with a revelation that nourishes the life He has given. Listen to His voice, to His word and to His call. In truth, there is no other!

Endnotes

Preface

[1] Oswald Chambers, *My Utmost for His Highest* (Discovery House Publishers, 1992), Feb. 10

Chapter Four

[1] John Calvin, *Gathered Gold* (Evangelical Press, 1984), p. 100
[2] George Meuller, *Gathered Gold* (Evangelical Press, 1984), p. 93

Chapter Nine

[1] A.W. Tozer, *The Knowledge of the Holy* (Harper & Row, Publishers Inc., 1961), p. 114

Chapter Ten

[1] John Pollock, *The Man Who Shook the World* (Victor Books, 1972)

Chapter Eleven

[1] C.S. Lewis, *Gathered Gold* (Evangelical Press, 1984), p. 194
[2] H.G. Wells, *Gathered Gold* (Evangelical Press, 1984), p. 194

Chapter Twelve

[1] Augustine of Hippo, *Gathered Gold* (Evangelical Press, 1984), p. 277

Chapter Fourteen

[1] David Otis Fuller, *Draper's Quotations for the Christian World via Quickverse Version 5* (Tyndale House Publishers, Inc. via Parsons Technology Inc., 1998)

[2] Edmund Burke, *Draper's Quotations for the Christian World via Quickverse Version 5* (Tyndale House Publishers, Inc. via Parsons Technology Inc., 1998)

Chapter Sixteen

[1] Robert Bateman, *An Artist in Nature* (Madison Press Limited, 1990), p. 157

Bibliography

Bateman, Robert. *An Artist in Nature*. Toronto: Madison Press Limited, 1990

Blanchard, John. *Gathered Gold*. Welwyn: Evangelical Press, 1984

Chambers, Oswald. *My Utmost for His Highest*. Nashville: Discovery House Publishers, 1992

Draper, Edythe. *Quotations for the Christian World*. Hiawatha: Parsons Technology Inc., 1998

Pollock, John. *The Man Who Shook the World*. Wheaton: Victor Books, 1972

Tozer, A.W. *The Knowledge of the Holy*. New York: Harper & Row Publishers, Inc., 1961

If any of these illustrations have inspired you
and you would like to order a print, please contact:
Robert M. Smith
Contract Art
robdeb@onlink.net
www.contract-art.com
(705) 752-4432